Reading Achievement
Comprehension Activities to Promote Essential Reading Skills

Grade 6

by
Darriel Ledbetter, M.S.
and
Leland Graham, Ph.D.

Table of Contents

Introduction

Welcome to the **Reading Achievement** series! Each book in this series is designed to reinforce the reading skills appropriate for each grade level and to encourage high-level thinking skills. Because reading is an essential part of all disciplines, mastery of these skills can help students succeed in all academic areas. In addition, experiencing success in reading can increase a student's self-esteem and motivate him or her to read more, both in and out of the classroom.

Each **Reading Achievement** book offers challenging questions for students to answer in response to a variety of grade-level appropriate passages. Various types of reading passages are represented in this book, including fiction, nonfiction, poetry, charts and graphs, and recipes. The format and questions are similar to those found on standardized reading tests. The experience students gain from answering questions in this format may help increase their test scores. In addition, these exercises can be used to enhance your school-adopted reading program, to individualize instruction, to provide extra practice for home schoolers, or to review skills between grades.

> The following reading skills are covered within this book:
>
> • **compare and contrast**
> • **comprehension**
> • **critical thinking**
> • **figurative language**
> • **following directions**
> • **main ideas/details**
> • **reference skills**
> • **sequencing**
> • **vocabulary**

Each **Reading Achievement** book contains additional features to enhance usability. Four pretests, in standardized test format, have been included at the beginning of each book. The pretests have been designed so that they may be used individually, as four stand-alone tests, or in groups. Another convenient feature is a scoring box on each activity page. This scoring box can be programmed to suit your specific classroom and student needs with total problems, total correct, and score.

Read the passage. Circle the letter beside each correct answer.

The 2000 Summer Olympics were held in Sydney, Australia. The country, which is also a continent, is about 3 million square miles of mostly flat, dry land. Australians, or "Aussies," call the interior area away from the coast, the outback. Few people live in the desert or semidesert land of the outback. Those who do live in "never-never land" often work on cattle and sheep ranches, called "stations." Stations are so big that helicopters and small planes are used to herd cattle and sheep and to check fences. Children who grow up in the outback often do not have neighbors, or nearby schools, so they learn from the *School of the Air.* They talk back and forth with their teachers by two-way radio! Medical help is available from the *Royal Flying Doctor Service,* which has airplane ambulances and clinics. Most Australians live in the coastal cities of the east, southeast, and southwest, like Sydney, Perth, Melbourne, and Brisbane.

1. The best title for this story is:
   A. The 2000 Summer Olympics
   C. Melbourne, Australia
   B. Living in the Australian Outback
   D. "Never-Never Land"

2. In this story, the expression "never-never land" means:
   A. a fairy tale
   C. an isolated area with few people
   B. a dream
   D. a large city

3. Students who live in the outback learn from the *School of the Air.* It is called this because:
   A. Airplanes drop books and assignments off for students.
   B. Students communicate with teachers on airwaves with two-way radios.
   C. Students communicate with teachers on the air over television.
   D. Students fly back and forth to school.

4. In the outback, small planes are used in the same way American ranchers use:
   A. bicycles
   C. radios
   B. trucks and four-wheel drive vehicles
   D. cars

5. If you were looking at a map of Australia, where would you find the outback?
   A. on the southwest coast
   C. on a mountain
   B. on the southeast coast
   D. in the center of the country

6. "Aussies" is a term that means:
   A. Australians
   C. olympians
   B. ranchers
   D. teachers

7. Which of the following sentences states an opinion?
   A. The 2000 Summer Olympics were held in Sydney, Australia.
   B. Australia covers about 3 million square miles of flat, dry land.
   C. Most Australians live in the coastal cities of the east, southeast, and southwest, like Sydney, Perth, Melbourne, and Brisbane.
   D. Australia is a fun place to live.

4

| Total Problems: | Total Correct: | Score: |

Read the passage. Circle the letter beside each correct answer.

For many students, entering sixth grade means leaving elementary school and entering middle school. A new school brings many new experiences and challenges, like dealing with lockers, changing classes, and meeting and making new friends. Following is some advice from former sixth graders that might make middle school easier.

- Sometimes teachers surprise you and take up your homework for a grade. Do your homework carefully and check over your answers. Doing this will save you a lot of bad grades.
- Don't write in pen in math class.
- You always have to be organized. If that means taking 10 minutes at night just to straighten up papers, then do it.
- Participate in school activities. Sign up for after school clubs or go out and support the football or track team. Don't come home in the afternoon and check your E-mail and go online. This just makes your friends and parents angry.
- Don't write down your homework assignments on your hand. Buy a little notebook and write them down there.
- If you can't get your locker open, get a teacher or friend to help you. Keep your lunch and library account numbers in your pocket. Don't tell everybody your locker combination.
- Don't worry about being popular. When you see the "popular" kids wearing name-brand clothes, don't think you have to wear those same brands just to be popular. Be yourself.

1. Advice about homework included all these except:
    A. Do your homework carefully.   B. Check over your answers.
    C. Write it down on your hand.   D. Write your assignments in a notebook.

2. What does one student advise you to do if you have trouble with your locker?
    A. Ask the principal for help.   B. Kick it.
    C. Cry.   D. Ask a friend or teacher for help.

3. Which of the following was not suggested as a way to make friends?
    A. Be yourself.   B. Participate in school activities.
    C. Check your E-mail every day.   D. Don't worry about being popular.

4. From the advice given, what might you conclude?
    A. All these students are popular.
    B. These students don't know what they are talking about.
    C. These students might have learned from making a mistake.
    D. These students always do what their parents tell them to.

5. What does one student suggest about being organized?
    A. It isn't important.   B. It guarantees better grades.
    C. It might take a few extra minutes.   D. It will make you more popular.

Total Problems:	Total Correct:	Score:

Name _____

Read each passage. Circle the letter beside the correct answer.

Ask a volunteer to write his age on a piece of paper without letting you see it. Then have him double this number. He then adds 5. Next he multiplies by 50 and subtracts 365. To this total have him add the total value of the change in his pockets, if it totals less than one dollar. Or have him add the number of coins he has (there must be fewer than 100). Now ask him the total. Then, you add 115 to the answer. The first two figures will show the person's age. The last two figures will give the value or number of coins that he is carrying.

1. In order for this trick to work, you must be able to:
   A. read minds
   C. add, subtract, and multiply
   B. multiply and divide
   D. see what is in someone's wallet

2. The volunteer completes how many arithmetic steps?
   A. 3
   B. 4
   C. 5
   D. 8

3. The third step that the volunteer completes is:
   A. doubles his age
   C. subtracts 365
   B. adds the change in his pocket
   D. adds five

4. What arithmetic must you do to complete the trick?
   A. Write down your age.
   C. Count the coins in his pocket.
   B. Add 115.
   D. Multiply by 365.

Turning a cartwheel is one of the basics of gymnastics, but it is harder than it looks. Before trying the steps suggested, take some safety precautions. Make sure a parent or some other adult is watching as the spotter. Use an exercise mat or something soft to land on. Make sure there's nothing around that will break or fall on you (outside is probably best).
- Stand in a lunge position, with your right leg forward and holding the left leg back. Put your hands straight in the air.
- Push off with your left foot and put your right hand on the floor. Your left leg follows in the air.
- Next, put your left hand on the floor followed by your right leg in the air.
- You should also finish in the lunge position. This time your left leg should be in front of you and your arms in the air. This position helps you to keep your balance.

5. In these directions, the "lunge" position means:
   A. with both feet together
   C. with one leg forward and one back
   B. with your feet shoulder-width apart
   D. on all fours

6. To start off, your hands should be:
   A. on your hips
   C. in your pockets
   B. on your shoulders
   D. in the air

7. Why is it important to finish in the lunge position?
   A. It helps you keep your balance.
   C. It keeps you from breaking something.
   B. It looks better.
   D. It is required by the gymnastics code.

6

Total Problems: _____   Total Correct: _____   Score: _____

Read the passage. Circle the letter beside each correct answer.

One morning some Canadian campers learned how smart a hungry squirrel can be. Every morning, the squirrel would come to find and carry away breakfast leftovers that the campers had left on a woodpile. The campers looked forward to this bit of entertainment each day. One day the little critter found a pancake too heavy for it to carry away. It pushed, pulled, and tugged as the campers watched and laughed. Suddenly, the squirrel stopped wrestling with the pancake and began to eat. He ate a hole in the center of the pancake and worked it over his head like a collar. Then, wearing this ruff, the squirrel dashed away to his favorite tree. Imagine the looks on the faces of the startled campers!

1. The best title for this story is:
    A.   A Crafty Critter
    C.   Camping Rules
    B.   A Lazy Squirrel
    D.   How to Dispose of Leftovers

2. In this story the word "critter" refers to:
    A.   a camper   B.   a squirrel   C.   a bear   D.   a gnat

3. What is the most likely setting for this story?
    A.   Colorado mountains
    C.   Canadian forest
    B.   Canadian seashore
    D.   California coast

4. From this story you could conclude that the campers saw the squirrel:
    A.   once a week
    C.   rarely
    B.   three times a day
    D.   each morning after breakfast

5. In this story, the word "ruff" means:
    A.   a collar
    C.   scratchy and prickly
    B.   the sound a dog makes
    D.   hard

6. From this story, you might guess that the pancake:
    A.   was a small "silver dollar" pancake
    C.   was much larger than the squirrel
    B.   was a blueberry pancake
    D.   was covered in syrup

7. From reading the story, how would you describe the squirrel?
    A.   not very smart
    C.   fat and lazy
    B.   persistent
    D.   slow

8. Why do you think the campers were startled at the squirrel's actions?
    A.   They didn't know he liked pancakes.
    B.   They didn't realize how smart a squirrel could be.
    C.   They just wanted to laugh at him.
    D.   They thought he would leave the pancake and come finish it later.

9. What word could you substitute for "smart" in the first sentence of this story?
    A.   sharp   B.   resourceful   C.   stylish   D.   sassy

Total Problems:	Total Correct:	Score:

7

Name _____ Pretest

Read the passage. Circle the letter beside each correct answer.

The 2000 Summer Olympics were held in Sydney, Australia. The country, which is also a continent, is about 3 million square miles of mostly flat, dry land. Australians, or "Aussies," call the interior area away from the coast, the outback. Few people live in the desert or semidesert land of the outback. Those who do live in "never-never land" often work on cattle and sheep ranches, called "stations." Stations are so big that helicopters and small planes are used to herd cattle and sheep and to check fences. Children who grow up in the outback often do not have neighbors, or nearby schools, so they learn from the *School of the Air*. They talk back and forth with their teachers by two-way radio! Medical help is available from the *Royal Flying Doctor Service*, which has airplane ambulances and clinics. Most Australians live in the coastal cities of the east, southeast, and southwest, like Sydney, Perth, Melbourne, and Brisbane.

1. The best title for this story is:
   A. The 2000 Summer Olympics   (B) Living in the Australian Outback
   C. Melbourne, Australia   D. "Never-Never Land"

2. In this story, the expression "never-never land" means:
   (A) a fairy tale   B. a dream
   (C) an isolated area with few people   D. a large city

3. Students who live in the outback learn from the *School of the Air*. It is called this because:
   A. Airplanes drop books and assignments off for students.
   (B) Students communicate with teachers on airwaves with two-way radios.
   C. Students communicate with teachers on the air over television.
   D. Students fly back and forth to school.

4. In the outback, small planes are used in the same way American ranchers use:
   A. bicycles   (B) trucks and four-wheel drive vehicles
   C. radios   D. cars

5. If you were looking at a map of Australia, where would you find the outback?
   A. on the southwest coast   B. on the southeast coast
   C. on a mountain   (D) in the center of the country

6. "Aussies" is a term that means:
   (A) Australians   B. ranchers
   C. olympians   D. teachers

7. Which of the following sentences states an opinion?
   A. The 2000 Summer Olympics were held in Sydney, Australia.
   B. Australia covers about 3 million square miles of flat, dry land.
   C. Most Australians live in the coastal cities of the east, southeast, and southwest, like Sydney, Perth, Melbourne, and Brisbane.
   (D) Australia is a fun place to live.

4 | Total Problems: ___ Total Correct: ___ Score: ___ | © Carson-Dellosa CD-2205

Name _____ Pretest

Read the passage. Circle the letter beside each correct answer.

For many students, entering sixth grade means leaving elementary school and entering middle school. A new school brings many new experiences and challenges, like dealing with lockers, changing classes, and meeting and making new friends. Following is some advice from former sixth graders that might make middle school easier.

- Sometimes teachers surprise you and take up your homework for a grade. Do your homework carefully and check over your answers. Doing this will save you a lot of bad grades.
- Don't write in pen in math class.
- You always have to be organized. If that means taking 10 minutes at night just to straighten up papers, then do it.
- Participate in school activities. Sign up for after school clubs or go out and support the football or track team. Don't come home in the afternoon and check your E-mail and go online. This just makes your friends and parents angry.
- Don't write down your homework assignments on your hand. Buy a little notebook and write them down there.
- If you can't get your locker open, get a teacher or friend to help you. Keep your lunch and library account numbers in your pocket. Don't tell everybody your locker combination.
- Don't worry about being popular. When you see the "popular" kids wearing name-brand clothes, don't think you have to wear those same brands just to be popular. Be yourself.

1. Advice about homework included all these except:
   A. Do your homework carefully.   B. Check over your answers.
   (C) Write it down on your hand.   D. Write your assignments in a notebook.

2. What does one student advise you to do if you have trouble with your locker?
   A. Ask the principal for help.   B. Kick it.
   C. Cry.   (D) Ask a friend or teacher for help.

3. Which of the following was not suggested as a way to make friends?
   A. Be yourself.   B. Participate in school activities.
   (C) Check your E-mail every day.   D. Don't worry about being popular.

4. From the advice given, what might you conclude?
   A. All these students are popular.
   B. These students don't know what they are talking about.
   (C) These students might have learned from making a mistake.
   D. These students always do what their parents tell them to.

5. What does one student suggest about being organized?
   A. It isn't important.   B. It guarantees better grades.
   (C) It might take a few extra minutes.   D. It will make you more popular.

© Carson-Dellosa CD-2205 | Total Problems: ___ Total Correct: ___ Score: ___ | **5**

Name _____ Pretest

Read each passage. Circle the letter beside the correct answer.

Ask a volunteer to write his age on a piece of paper without letting you see it. Then have him double this number. He then adds 5. Next he multiplies by 50 and subtracts 365. To this total have him add the total value of the change in his pockets, if it totals less than one dollar. Or have him add the number of coins he has (there must be fewer than 100). Now ask him the total. Then, you add 115 to the answer. The first two figures will show the person's age. The last two figures will give the value or number of coins that he is carrying.

1. In order for this trick to work, you must be able to:
   (A) read minds   B. multiply and divide
   (C) add, subtract, and multiply   D. see what is in someone's wallet

2. The volunteer completes how many arithmetic steps?
   A. 3   B. 4   C. 5   (D) 8

3. The third step that the volunteer completes is:
   A. doubles his age   B. adds the change in his pocket
   C. subtracts 365   (D) adds five

4. What arithmetic must you do to complete the trick?
   A. Write down your age.   (B) Add 115.
   C. Count the coins in his pocket.   D. Multiply by 365.

Turning a cartwheel is one of the basics of gymnastics, but it is harder than it looks. Before trying the steps suggested, take some safety precautions. Make sure a parent or some other adult is watching as the spotter. Use an exercise mat or something soft to land on. Make sure there's nothing around that will break or fall on you (outside is probably best).
- Stand in a lunge position, with your right leg forward and holding the left leg back. Put your hands straight in the air.
- Push off with your left foot and put your right hand on the floor. Your left leg follows in the air.
- Next, put your left hand on the floor followed by your right leg in the air.
- You should also finish in the lunge position. This time your left leg should be in front of you and your arms in the air. This position helps you to keep your balance.

5. In these directions, the "lunge" position means:
   A. with both feet together   B. with your feet shoulder-width apart
   (C) with one leg forward and one back   D. on all fours

6. To start off, your hands should be:
   A. on your hips   B. on your shoulders
   C. in your pockets   (D) in the air

7. Why is it important to finish in the lunge position?
   (A) It helps you keep your balance.   B. It looks better.
   C. It keeps you from breaking something.   D. It is required by the gymnastics code.

6 | Total Problems: ___ Total Correct: ___ Score: ___ | © Carson-Dellosa CD-2205

Name _____ Pretest

Read the passage. Circle the letter beside each correct answer.

One morning some Canadian campers learned how smart a hungry squirrel can be. Every morning, the squirrel would come to find and carry away breakfast leftovers that the campers had left on a woodpile. The campers looked forward to this bit of entertainment each day. One day the little critter found a pancake too heavy for it to carry away. It pushed, pulled, and tugged as the campers watched and laughed. Suddenly, the squirrel stopped wrestling with the pancake and began to eat. He ate a hole in the center of the pancake and worked it over his head like a collar. Then, wearing this ruff, the squirrel dashed away to his favorite tree. Imagine the looks on the faces of the startled campers!

1. The best title for this story is:
   (A) A Crafty Critter   B. A Lazy Squirrel
   C. Camping Rules   D. How to Dispose of Leftovers

2. In this story the word "critter" refers to:
   A. a camper   (B) a squirrel   C. a bear   D. a gnat

3. What is the most likely setting for this story?
   A. Colorado mountains   B. Canadian seashore
   (C) Canadian forest   D. California coast

4. From this story you could conclude that the campers saw the squirrel:
   A. once a week   B. three times a day
   C. rarely   (D) each morning after breakfast

5. In this story, the word "ruff" means:
   (A) a collar   B. the sound a dog makes
   C. scratchy and prickly   D. hard

6. From this story, you might guess that the pancake:
   A. was a small "silver dollar" pancake   B. was a blueberry pancake
   (C) was much larger than the squirrel   D. was covered in syrup

7. From reading the story, how would you describe the squirrel?
   A. not very smart   (B) persistent
   C. fat and lazy   D. slow

8. Why do you think the campers were startled at the squirrel's actions?
   A. They didn't know he liked pancakes.
   (B) They didn't realize how smart a squirrel could be.
   C. They just wanted to laugh at him.
   D. They thought he would leave the pancake and come finish it later.

9. What word could you substitute for "smart" in the first sentence of this story?
   A. sharp   (B) resourceful   C. stylish   D. sassy

© Carson-Dellosa CD-2205 | Total Problems: ___ Total Correct: ___ Score: ___ | **7**

Read each question and circle the letter beside the correct answer.

1.   An inference one can make is that:
     A.   Grandpa has recovered and is ready to go fishing again.
     B.   Aunt Molly and Meg are worried about Billy.
     C.   The weather was beautiful on the morning of their fishing trip.
     D.   Billy's mother is angry at him.

2.   The word "cooperate," in the seventh paragraph, means:
     A.   go fishing
     B.   listen
     C.   dive into the water
     D.   argue

3.   The doctor told Aunt Molly and Meg to:
     A.   give Billy fluids   B.   be patient
     C.   call Billy's friends   D.   take Billy fishing

4.   After reading the seventh paragraph, one can draw the conclusion that:
     A.   Grandpa was knocked overboard by the crashing waves.
     B.   Billy dropped the anchor into the water.
     C.   A large fish had jumped out of, and back into, the water.
     D.   The boat flipped over and dumped everyone into the water.

5.   How does Billy cope with the boating accident?
     A.   He visits Grandpa every day in the hospital.
     B.   He discusses with Aunt Molly what happened.
     C.   He has blocked the accident from his mind.
     D.   He gets up every morning and has breakfast just as he normally would.

6.   How was the weather the day of the accident?
     A.   It was a beautiful afternoon.   B.   There was a storm in the morning.
     C.   It was a beautiful day.   D.   There was a storm in the afternoon.

7.   What is Billy doing as the story opens?
     A.   visiting Grandpa   B.   staring out the window
     C.   eating breakfast   D.   getting prepared to fish

Total Problems: **Total Correct:**   **Score:**   **29**

Read the passage and answer the questions on the following page.

Why Dolphins Jump Out of the Water

A long time ago on a bright afternoon, Sunny was feeling very sad. Moony asked, "What is wrong with you today, Sunny?"

Sunny replied, "I am tired of doing the same thing every day. I want an adventure."

To this Moony said, "I know a place that is very dark and needs sunshine."

"Where?" Sunny responded.

"The ocean," said Moony.

The next day Sunny said good-bye to all of his heavenly friends and fell from the sky with a big splash. Creating such a huge disturbance caused the animals in the sea to avoid Sunny. The animals swam away as quickly as possible, making Sunny very sad. What was Sunny going to do?

Toby, a brave dolphin, decided to investigate the disturbance and the intruder. After a lengthy conversation with Sunny, Toby learned that Sunny was nice and just wanted to be friends with everyone. Without waiting too long, Toby called all the fish and other dolphins together to meet Sunny.

The animals loved Sunny and spent hours playing together in their new lighted underworld. At first, everyone was excited to have light in their world under the ocean. But Bob, the king of the ocean, noticed after a few days that some of the plants and animals had actually begun to die. Sunny did not know why, but Bob did. Bob explained that many plants and animals in the ocean are accustomed to cold temperatures and no light. Now that Sunny was there, the temperature was warmer and there was much light.

Bob decided he would have to ask Sunny to leave. Sunny loved his new life and friends in the ocean and did not want to leave. Finally, Bob said, "Sunny, if you don't leave, the ocean will die. We do love you very much, but we can't survive if you stay."

After a minute, Sunny said, "Bob, I will leave, but may I stay one more night to say good-bye to all my friends?" Bob agreed that Sunny could stay one more night.

The next day, after saying a tearful good-bye to everyone, Sunny left. Before Sunny left, however, Toby told his new friend that he would never forget him. As a reminder of their friendship, Toby said he would occasionally jump out of the water into the light to say "hi" to Sunny in the sky.

With tears in his eyes, Sunny returned home to find Moony waiting and watching. Moony wanted to know everything about the trip into the ocean and all the friends Sunny had made. Furthermore, Moony said one day he might have to travel into the ocean to meet all of Sunny's friends. In the meantime, sometimes during the day or night, Moony can see a dolphin jumping out of the ocean with Sunny looking on and smiling.

Answer the questions below. Circle the letter beside the correct answer where appropriate.

1. Arrange the sentences in chronological order, from 1 to 6.

    _____ Toby called all the fish and dolphins together.

    _____ Sunny wanted an adventure.

    _____ Bob decided to ask Sunny to leave.

    _____ Moony can see a dolphin jumping out of the ocean.

    _____ All the animals swam away as quickly as possible.

    _____ Toby said he would occasionally jump out of the water.

2. Who was the "king of the ocean"?
    A. Toby   B. Bob
    C. Sunny   D. Moony

3. The names Sunny and Moony represent the sun and the moon. Therefore, the names are:
    A. similes   B. metaphors
    C. symbols   D. alliterative

4. Why did Sunny want to visit the ocean?
    A. He wanted to fish.   B. He wanted a drink of water.
    C. He didn't want any friends. D. He wanted an adventure.

5. What can you infer from reading the story?
    A. Moony liked it when Sunny was away.
    B. Sunny does not belong in the sky; instead, Sunny belongs in the ocean.
    C. Bob, the king of the ocean, was mean to Sunny by asking Sunny to leave.
    D. Animals in the ocean cannot adapt to new, contrasting conditions without any problems.

6. The main idea of this story is:
    A. Some plants in the ocean need light to grow.
    B. Sunny wanted to make friends with all the people on earth.
    C. Everything has its role or function in the world.
    D. Dolphins, on occasion, jump out of the water.

Total Problems:	Total Correct:	Score:

Read the passage and answer the questions on the following page.

Soccer Star

Once upon a time, in a small town in South Dakota, there lived a small boy. This little boy's name was Gunther. Gunther was different from all the other kids at his school because he was so much smaller than everyone else. At the primary and elementary schools, he was taunted and teased by the other kids because he was shorter and skinnier.

When Gunther went to the middle school, he found that the students were the same to him there as they were at the other schools; however, as the school year progressed, he began to grow little by little. Before his sixth grade year was over, he was almost as tall as the other kids in his class. No one hardly ever made fun of him anymore.

Then, soccer tryouts came around in the spring, and Gunther decided he would try out for the team. All the bigger boys that had been on the team before just laughed at him and began to make fun of him again. This naturally pushed Gunther to try harder to show the coach just what he could do. After a few weeks of running and working out, Gunther was in good condition.

During the first soccer game, the star player twisted his ankle, and the coach had to put Gunther in the game. None of the other players thought he would do well. On the first play, Gunther captured the ball and kicked a goal. The crowd cheered wildly for him. As Gunther ran down the field, the other players blocked for him and were amazed at his speed and agility. Finally, Gunther made the winning goal, and his teammates carried him off the field.

Gunther was cheered by the fans and his teammates after the game. For once in his life, he felt special. From that moment on, he was never made fun of again. He was considered a hero for being the player who scored the winning goal in the game against his school's arch rival.

Read each question and circle the letter beside the correct answer.

1. The main idea of the story is:
   A. Soccer is a fun sport for all young boys.
   B. One should never give up, regardless of size and stature.
   C. One should always fight back.
   D. School can be a great place for learning new ideas.

2. Another word or expression that means the same as "agility" is:
   A. helpless
   B. angry
   C. slow
   D. ability to move quickly

3. Which event occurred last in the story?
   A. He was taunted and teased by the other kids.
   B. He was never made fun of again.
   C. Gunther decided he would try out for the team.
   D. He found that the students were the same to him there.

4. What conclusion can you draw from the story?
   A. If one tries and never gives up, things will work out for the best.
   B. If one is short, then eating a lot of food will help one to grow taller.
   C. Soccer is more fun to play than football.
   D. Sixth grade is more challenging than any other grade.

5. Why was Gunther taunted and teased by the students?
   A. He was from a foreign country.
   B. He was an A student.
   C. He was shorter than most children his age.
   D. His family was poor.

6. What mishap occurred that enabled Gunther to play in the first game?
   A. The star player was involved in a car accident on his way to the game.
   B. The star player slipped and fell in the locker room.
   C. The star player was suspended because of poor grades.
   D. The star player twisted his ankle.

Total Problems:	Total Correct:	Score:

Read the passage and answer the questions on the following page.

A Cow Tale

Once upon a time, in a pasture far, far away there was a very disgruntled dairy cow. Clarabel was forced to work as a milk producer and was given very little time to enjoy even the little things in her life. She envied the other cows that just sat around all day eating and sleeping without a care in the world, or so she thought. If only she could change pastures, her life would greatly improve, but it seemed impossible. You see, Clarabel was a black and white spotted cow while the other cows were all brown with white faces. There was no way she could go against this obvious show of shameful bigotry. She had to come up with a plan.

Early one morning, it began to rain very hard in the pasture. Unfortunately, Clarabel was very thirsty and would have to walk to the other side of the pasture to get to the pond. She believed the rainwater to be impure and was sure it would lessen her spots. As she was approaching the water, she became weary because of the slippery grass. Then it happened; she slipped and fell into a huge, mud puddle. Horrified, she just lay there until after the rain had ceased. When she stood up, she was covered in mud from head to toe, completely brown except for a small spot on her face. At first, she was going to take a running leap into the pond to wash off the mud. Then it came to her—she looked like one of the cows from the next pasture.

Immediately, Clarabel had to get the attention of one of the neighboring ranchers. She moved as close as possible to the next pasture and began mooing as loudly as she could. This prompted one of the ranchers to come over to the fence. As he screamed and hollered something about "cow thieves" and "police," she was quickly led out of the fence and into the pasture she had been wanting to join for so long. She began trying to make friends with her new pasture pals. Clarabel had always had a very easy time making friends, but these cows seemed to have something on their minds. At nightfall, they all huddled in a circle in the center of the pasture and began to sing sad moo songs, while gently swaying back and forth. They kept saying something about "the burden of beef" and "fast food will be the end of us all." None of this made any sense to Clarabel, and it seemed that everyone was too occupied with these threats to explain them to her. Confused, Clarabel decided to go to sleep and worry about it in the morning.

When Clarabel awoke the next morning, she noticed all her fellow cows were being herded into big trucks and taken away. She was an intelligent cow and had managed somehow to learn to read a little. The trucks had words written on them about beef and hamburger. She was not familiar with either of these words and strained her ears to listen to the other cows. They were yelling at her saying, "run while you can" and "save yourself." It became apparent that for whatever reason these cows would not be returning.

Although she began running away, Clarabel soon ended up on a separate, smaller truck. Clarabel realized her truck was going toward her old pasture, the opposite direction from the others. When she arrived, she literally ran off the ramp and into her beloved pasture. Somehow she had been recognized and saved. As she walked up to the pond, she saw her reflection. All the mud was gone; it must have rained during the night. From that point on, Clarabel was glad to be a dairy cow and danced and mooed every time it rained.

34

Name _____

Read the questions below. Circle the letter beside the correct answer where appropriate.

1. Arrange the sentences in chronological order, from 1 to 6.

   _____ They all huddled in a circle in the center of the pasture and began to sing.

   _____ She literally ran off the ramp and into her beloved pasture.

   _____ Then it happened; she slipped and fell into a huge mud puddle.

   _____ They were yelling at her, saying, "run while you can" and "save yourself."

   _____ If only she could change pastures, her life would greatly improve.

   _____ She moved as close as possible to the next pasture and began mooing.

2. The main idea of the story is:
   A. Cows should be allowed to enjoy themselves.
   B. You should be satisfied with what you have.
   C. Dairy cows lead a hard life.
   D. A cow is just like a human.

3. In the last paragraph, Clarabel "walked up to the pond" and ". . . she saw her reflection." What inference can you make concerning why Clarabel was not taken on the trucks with the other cows?
   A. Clarabel was a cow with special privileges.
   B. The trucks were full and had no more room for Clarabel.
   C. The farmer did not want to get rid of Clarabel.
   D. Only brown cows with white faces were taken away in trucks.

4. Choose the expression below which portrays "bigotry."
   A. placing two cows of the same breed into two different pastures with equal portions
   B. giving special privileges to a cow who is brown and white, not black and white
   C. recognizing that one cow is bigger than another cow
   D. placing two cows in one pasture and three cows in another pasture

Total Problems:	Total Correct:	Score:

Read the passage and answer the questions that follow. Circle the letter beside each correct answer.

Pieces of Life

Thinking of her daughter as a child again, an old woman sits in her chair with her quilting supplies beside her. She places her wrinkled hand into a woven basket where many different colorful pieces of clothes lay. She reaches to the bottom to find her most precious possession. As she brings it into her lap, a tear gently runs down her wrinkled face. As she holds her double-ringed quilt in her trembling hands, memories of each piece begin to fill her with emotions. She glides her hands over each piece, as if she were remembering each minute of her life. Now she must piece together a new quilt because her youngest daughter will soon be married. Not only does this particular double-ringed quilt represent the unity of a man and woman, but it also represents a summary of her daughter's life.

Picking up the first piece of a dress, she remembers the day her little girl wore this home from the hospital. As each piece brings more memories, the old mother bonds them together, using the threads of life. These threads connect each day within the daughter's life, as well as her mother's life. As she sews the pieces of different garments together, she knows that her daughter will do this one day. The tradition of making quilts will continue because it represents her job of helping to piece memories of her children's lives together.

1. In the second paragraph, what does the expression "threads of life" mean?
     A.   the way the old woman and her children's lives and the quilt are intertwined
     B.   the way her daughter has spent her life
     C.   memories of how she and her husband spent their lives
     D.   represents all the spools of thread she has purchased

2. What evidence supports the expression in the first line "an old woman"?
     A.   has several children
     B.   making a quilt
     C.   wrinkled hands and face
     D.   she reminisces

3. In the last line, ". . . to piece her children's lives together" means:
     A.   The old woman is sewing pieces of quilt patterns together.
     B.   The old woman is sewing memories of her family into the quilt.
     C.   The old woman is using a photo album to recall her children's lives.
     D.   The old woman is trying to understand her children's behavior.

Total Problems: _____   Total Correct: _____   Score: _____

Read the passage and answer the questions that follow. Circle the letter beside each correct answer.

Woolby

It was quiet. The sun had already gone down over the horizon, and a big, beautiful harvest moon could be seen. It was still mostly dark, though. All I could see were the shadowy outlines of the objects around me, and any movement would let them know I was there. I had my mission, and there was nothing that was going to keep me from completing it.

I decided to lay low and not make any move until just before 9:00. I had to go about 200 yards across the field in front of me to get to where I needed to be. I looked up and could see many bright lights. That was my goal, and I knew that getting there was going to be difficult.

I could tell that soon it was going to be closing time. I decided that I would have to make my move in a few minutes. Suddenly, acting on instinct, I leapt forward and began to run to the glimmers of light in the distance. I was sprinting across the open area at full speed weaving and dodging the enemy left and right. Children were counting on me, and I was not going to let them down.

Reaching the doorway of the building, inside where I wanted to be, I quickly made my way. Inside, I continued to run as I went down a long narrow aisle with all kinds of things on shelves on each side. I was sure the personnel were watching me, I was sure, but I had to make it to the package before I was led outside. As I turned the aisle, I saw it lying there. I grabbed it and ran in the direction from which I had come.

As I reached my destination and placed the package on the counter, she looked at me and then said, "Sir, would you like to pay cash, or charge your Woolby?"

1. Possibly, in what kind of store is the narrator?
    A. grocery store   B. clothing store
    C. toy store   D. travel agency

2. The "personnel" in the fourth paragraph could be:
    A. teachers   B. doctors
    C. the sixth grade class   D. sales clerks

3. "Charge your Woolby" means:
    A. Place a stamp on it.   B. Pay for the Woolby with a charge card.
    C. Attack the Woolby.   D. Change its looks.

4. In the first paragraph, the narrator states, "I had my mission." What is the mission?
    A. to enter the store before closing time and return a Woolby
    B. to enter the store before closing time and attack a Woolby
    C. to enter the store before closing time and purchase a Woolby
    D. to enter the store before closing time and steal a Woolby

Read the passage and answer the questions on the following page.

Nails

Once upon a time there was a very small, but unusual kitten named Nails. He was the smallest of the litter, but that did not seem to bother him at all. Nails was unusual because he was the only cat around that had such long nails, almost twice the length of most cats' nails.

One day, he and his family decided to take a short journey to town to visit Nails' Uncle Bob. Laughing and playing, everyone was having a swell time along the way, including Nails who stopped to chase a butterfly that had attracted his attention. However, this distraction caused Nails to fall well behind his family, who continued on the way to town and Uncle Bob's house.

After finally catching the big black and yellow butterfly, Nails realized his family had left him behind, probably not realizing he wasn't with them. "Oh no! How am I going to find my family?" he exclaimed to the butterfly, whose name was Billy.

"I can help you find your family if you will let me go," said Billy, after noticing that Nails was almost in a state of panic. Nails agreed and the two were off in hopes of finding the family.

Of course, this was no ordinary butterfly. He was quite intelligent, as intelligent as Albert Einstein, and he certainly knew his way around. Billy was very observant, too. He couldn't help but notice Nails' strange paws with the long nails. These nails were unlike any he had ever seen before. Billy couldn't resist asking, "Why are your nails so long? I've never seen any that long."

Nails replied, "I really do not know, but my mom has always told me they will come in handy one day." So Nails and Billy continued their search, with Billy directing the way. Soon, they came to a stream that had flooded its banks. Cats, of course, hate to get wet, so at the first sight of water, Nails stopped dead in his tracks. Billy asked, "What is wrong with you, little buddy?"

"Don't you know that cats hate water?" Nails responded in a voice that seemed angry and scared. Understanding Nails' fear now, Billy looked up and down the stream. He hoped he could find a very narrow stretch in the stream where they could cross. After looking for a short time, he didn't find a narrow stretch, but he did find a long tree that had fallen across the stream. "This will make a good bridge, and we can cross here," Billy said to Nails, who was waiting and watching.

Gathering his courage, Nails finally started across the crude bridge. He had gone about eight feet when he slipped. Billy yelled from above him, "Nails, are you all right?"

"I think so, but I can't do this. I want to back up," said Nails, again with disgust and fright in his voice. By this time, Nails was very scared and almost in tears.

Knowing this tree bridge was the only way to cross the stream, Billy said, "Use your long nails to hold onto the tree and go slowly across the log. It is the only way for you to find your family. You can do it, so trust yourself." Hesitating, Nails held his breath as he held on tightly to the log and began to creep across it. Slowly, he crawled to the other side, with Billy above, directing and encouraging him.

Read each question. Circle the letter beside the correct answer.

1. The main idea of the short story is:
   A. Long toenails are good things to have.
   B. Don't chase butterflies alone in the woods.
   C. Never give up and rely on your inner strength as well as your physical strength.
   D. Don't talk with strangers if your parents aren't around.

2. Where was Nails going when he suddenly became lost and disoriented?
   A. to get groceries
   B. to visit Uncle Bob in town
   C. to find Billy
   D. to play in the stream

3. What was the first question Billy asked Nails after their initial meeting?
   A. I can help you find your family if you will let me go.
   B. How am I going to find my family?
   C. What is wrong with you, little buddy?
   D. Why are your nails so long?

4. Which statement is false?
   A. Billy was an ordinary butterfly.
   B. Billy was an intelligent butterfly.
   C. Billy was a butterfly that could talk.
   D. Billy knew his way around in the forest.

5. Why was Nails afraid to cross the tree log that had fallen across the stream?
   A. Nails was afraid of heights and trees.
   B. Cats do not like to get wet.
   C. Nails was just a beginner swimmer, and he was afraid he might fall into the water.
   D. Nails did not trust Billy; he thought Billy would push him into the water.

6. What color was Billy?
   A. black and white
   B. yellow and brown
   C. yellow and black
   D. black and purple

7. What conclusion can you draw after reading the story of Nails?
   A. From now on, Nails will never chase another butterfly as long as he lives.
   B. From now on, Nails will never travel anywhere without his parents.
   C. From now on, Nails will be swimming in the stream every day.
   D. From now on, Nails probably will have more confidence in himself.

8. "He (Billy) was quite intelligent, as intelligent as Albert Einstein," is an example of:
   A. a simile
   B. a pun
   C. a metaphor
   D. a personification

Total Problems:	Total Correct:	Score:

Read the passage and answer the questions that follow. Circle the letter beside the correct answer.

How Time Flies

Close your eyes. Count to ten. Now open your eyes. That is almost how quickly life can pass you by. Just yesterday, it seems, the most important thing in the world to me was mastering the art of riding a bicycle. If I could just learn how, I thought, then everything would be right in the world. When I finally learned, happiness was all around me, covering me like a protective bubble. How quickly things change. Now, I hardly remember the last time I even sat on a bicycle.

The things that had once been so important, now seem trifles, and there is hardly time even to think of them, much less enjoy them. There is no time for the long ago, warm summer days on the back porch with watermelon juice from head to toe, and no time to roll and tumble in a field of newly cut hay. There is no time to take a short hike in the woods, to plant a little flower bed in the spring, to help my dad mow and rake the lawn on a summer day, or to climb a tree and swing down again.

Oh, how I took those days for granted. If only I had known they would go by so quickly. Rarely is there time to reflect and remember. It seems life always has me by the collar, pulling me in one direction or the other. I was so carefree in elementary and middle school, but now in high school with clubs, extracurricular activities, homework, chores at home, friends, and my part-time job, I seem to be too busy.

Maybe today I will go outside and ride my bike. I think I still know how to do it. Today is going to be my day. I am going to ride my bike, smell the air, climb a tree, and just sit there and think.

1. In the first paragraph, "happiness was all around me, covering me like a protective bubble." The word "happiness" is compared to:
   A. me   B. a covering
   C. a bubble   D. a bicycle

2. Approximately how old is the writer in the above passage?
   A. 20-25 years old   B. 15-18 years old
   C. 7-12 years old   D. 30-35 years old

3. The main idea in the passage above is:
   A. Sometimes we may take life for granted.
   B. Growing up now is difficult for teenagers.
   C. Everyone should learn to ride a bicycle.
   D. The older you get, the more you enjoy sports.

Total Problems:	Total Correct:	Score:

Read the passage and answer the questions that follow. Circle the letter beside the correct answer.

Brown Coat Angel

A boy and a few of his friends were in the woods playing a game of "capture the flag." They were having a great time. Suddenly, there was a clap of thunder like the sound of his grandfather's hammer. Rain began to fall between the cracks in the canopy of the forest. All of the boys began to hurry home in hopes that they would not get too wet. However, one boy tripped over a log and fell into a steep-sided creek. None of the others even noticed.

The rain began to fall harder and harder. The boy who was left behind was totally drenched. During his fall, he had sprained his ankle and could not climb out. He could feel the pain pulsing through his foot, but he tried to ignore it. He reached for a big stick that was lying near him and used it to help raise himself.

Just as the boy grabbed the stick, he heard some leaves rustling nearby. He turned his head and saw a man standing there. Wearing a long brown coat, the bearded man was tall and possibly in his late thirties. The stranger reached down and helped the young boy out of the creek. Once they reached the boy's house, the rain had stopped. The boy was glad to see his parents and turned around to thank the man. As he looked back, the boy saw nothing but the horizon in the distance.

1. A conclusion you could draw from the passage is:
   A. One should not play alone in the woods.
   B. The boy was helped by an angel.
   C. Playing "capture the flag" can be fun.
   D. One should avoid the outdoors during a lightning storm.

2. "There was a clap of thunder like the sound of his grandfather's hammer." The clap of thunder is compared to the sound of his grandfather's hammer. This writing technique is called:
   A. pun
   B. metaphor
   C. simile
   D. personification

Read the passage and answer the questions on the following page.

Waiting Her Whole Life

It seemed that Claire had been waiting her whole life for this day. However, in reality, it had been only five months since she had met John. It was possible that it seemed longer because from the moment she met him, her life had changed. From the first moment of their meeting, she had been waiting for this date to come. There was one thing for sure. She certainly had not realized that it would take so much work. Those who had done this before had told her it would be difficult at times, but Claire had smiled in self-assurance. She just knew it would be different for John and her. But her self-assurance turned out to be only the inexperience of her youth.

As the final days drew near, there was so much to do to make everything perfect. Claire spent many sleepless nights tossing and turning, too worried to sleep. Some nights she did not even make it to her bed. She was up all night preparing for the big day. The sleepless nights would sometimes result in Claire becoming very emotional around John, and this concerned him. Claire was certain that he was making the process more difficult than it should be, but John had his own peculiar ways and ideas.

When the day finally came, it was a beautiful spring morning. The air was so fresh and bright. Claire was nervous, but at the same time in a state of perfect bliss. It was to begin at 11:00 A.M. She walked slowly through the crowd of students, knowing that at the end of her walk, John would be there, waiting on her. Still, she was a little worried. There were so many details to remember. Had she done everything she needed to do to be prepared?

In retrospect, Claire could not see how she had ever made it through that hour and a half, but somehow she did. It lasted longer than she had wanted—ending at 12:15. Relieved and anxious, she was finally able to walk out to the sound of the ringing bell. Turning to her friend, she said, "Thank goodness, I'm through with chemistry for the semester. I hope I didn't fail that final. Come on, Amanda. Let's get some lunch. I'm starved."

Read each question. Circle the letter beside the correct question.

1. The story is about Claire and:
    A.   John on their wedding day
    B.   John on their first date
    C.   her chemistry semester test
    D.   Amanda on their first day in high school

2. Another word or expression for "retrospect," in the last paragraph, is:
    A.   inspection   B.   the past
    C.   looking back   D.   the present

3. One can draw the conclusion that John is the:
    A.   future husband   B.   best friend's brother
    C.   date   D.   teacher

4. In the first paragraph, the expression "Those who had done this before had told her it would be difficult at times" means:
    A.   Those who had planned a wedding before had found the preparations sometimes difficult and stressful.
    B.   Those who had gone out on their first date would find the experience difficult and stressful.
    C.   Those who had taken chemistry before had found the course to be difficult.
    D.   Those who had met Amanda had found her to be difficult at times.

5. One can conclude that Claire is in high school because:
    A.   She is taking a chemistry class.   B.   She has her first date.
    C.   She is nervous.   D.   She has much homework.

6. Which one of the following happened first?
    A.   Let's get some lunch.
    B.   Claire spent many sleepless nights tossing and turning.
    C.   She walked slowly through the crowd of people.
    D.   She was finally able to walk out to the sound of the ringing bell.

Total Problems:	Total Correct:	Score:

Read the passage and answer the questions that follow. Circle the letter beside the correct answer.

The Tree House

Jan was sitting on the bottom step of her tree house ladder. Although it was a bitter autumn day, she was not wearing a coat because coats were for babies. Her best friend Belinda was wearing a new burgundy sweater that her aunt had bought her the day before. Because the air was cutting their lungs, they decided to go up into the old tree house. The tree house had been built eleven years ago when Jan turned one year old. Since then, she had painted it every summer and kept it fairly clean. The roof was black and the outer walls a very light sky blue. The ladder was brown and twisted like a screw. The one big room had brown carpet so that dirt would not show as much. Over the years, the girls had added furniture to the house. There was a small rocking chair that was handed down from Jan's grandmother, a coffee table, and a beanbag chair in the corner. When they spent the weekends together, the tree house was like a home to Jan and Belinda. The house was also a place where they could get away from everyone and sort out their problems.

1.   The one big room in the tree house is described as having:
     A.   a beanbag chair, rocking chair, black carpet, and a coffee table
     B.   a rocking chair, beanbag chair, brown carpet, and an end table
     C.   a beanbag chair, brown carpet, a rocking chair, and a coffee table
     D.   a coffee table, brown carpet, beanbag chair, and a straight chair

2.   "The ladder was brown and twisted like a screw." In this sentence, the ladder is compared to a:
     A.   brown color
     B.   screw
     C.   twist
     D.   not given

3.   "The house had been built eleven years ago when Jan turned one year old." How old is Jan now?
     A.   11 years old
     B.   13 years old
     C.   10 years old
     D.   12 years old

Total Problems:	Total Correct:	Score:

Read the passage and answer the questions that follow. Circle the letter beside the correct answer.

Writing an Essay

Writing an essay or composition can be easy and fun if you follow a few procedures. First, write a relatively short introduction of three to four sentences. The purpose of the opening paragraph is to introduce the topic to the reader. The thesis statement or main idea of the whole paper is found in the introduction, and is usually the last sentence.

The next major part of the essay is called the supporting paragraphs. You should have at least two supporting paragraphs with at least five sentences in each paragraph. Each supporting paragraph begins with a topic sentence, which introduces the main idea for that paragraph. Supporting paragraphs contain details, facts, examples, passages, and quotes that support or reinforce your thesis statement.

The last major part of the essay is called the concluding paragraph. This last paragraph is also short—maybe three or four sentences. The purpose of the concluding paragraph is to bring the essay to a close. The first sentence is the restated thesis statement in which you write your thesis statement again, but in different words. The idea here is to bring the whole paper back together, to refocus and conclude.

1. The last part of the essay is called the:
   A.   supporting paragraphs
   B.   concluding paragraph
   C.   thesis statement
   D.   introduction

2. Each supporting paragraph contains:
   A.   three sentences
   B.   a thesis statement
   C.   a topic sentence
   D.   a restated thesis statement

3. An essay contains how many major parts?
   A.   3   B.   2
   C.   4   D.   5

4. Supporting paragraphs contain all but one of the following:
   A.   facts   B.   examples
   C.   details   D.   a thesis statement

Total Problems:	Total Correct:	Score:

Read the passage and answer the questions on the following page.

Canada: A Parliamentary Democracy

Canada is a parliamentary democracy. The country has a national legislature called Parliament, which meets in Ottawa, the national capital. The Canadian Parliament is composed of the House of Commons and the Senate. Representatives of the lower house, the House of Commons, are elected. Members of the upper house, the Senate, are appointed by the governor general.

The leader of Canada's national government is the prime minister. A prime minister is the leader of the political party that has a majority of members in the House of Commons. A majority is more than half the total number.

In Canada, the prime minister heads both the executive and the legislative branches of government. The two branches are not separate in Canada as they are in the United States. The prime minister governs with the help of the cabinet. The cabinet is comprised of the prime minister and about 30 members of the House of Commons. The cabinet members advise the prime minister and help him or her carry out the law.

The principle political parties include the Liberal Party, the Progressive Conservative Party, and the New Democratic Party. The major regional parties include the British Columbia Social Credit Party and the Parti Quebecois—important mainly in Quebec. Some prime ministers include Pierre Trudeau, from 1968-1979 and 1980-1984, and Brian Mulroney, from 1984-1988.

The prime minister depends on the support of Parliament to stay in office. Without the support from Parliament, the prime minister must resign. A prime minister did resign after several events in 1988, when important members of the government were criticized for "betraying the people."

Canada is one of the members of the Commonwealth of Nations, a group of independent nations once ruled by Great Britain. Commonwealth nations think of the British monarch—the king or queen—as the head of their governments. A monarchy is any government headed by a hereditary ruler, such as a king or queen. However, in Canada the British monarch is the leader in name only.

In Canada, the British monarch is represented by an official called the governor general. The governor general has little power. For the most part, this official approves decisions made by Parliament and the prime minister.

Answer the questions below. Circle the letter beside the correct answer if appropriate.

1.   The main idea of the descriptive passage is that:
     A.   Brian Mulroney was the best prime minister in Canada's history.
     B.   Canada has a very strict monarchy headed by Pierre Trudeau.
     C.   Canada has a parliamentary democracy.
     D.   The prime minister advises the cabinet members in carrying out the law.

2.   The Canadian Parliament is composed of which two branches of government?
     A.   Senate and House of Commons
     B.   Senate and Liberal Party
     C.   Parti Quebecois and Congress
     D.   House of Representatives and Senate

3.   A "monarchy" is:
     A.   any government headed by a prime minister
     B.   any government headed by a president
     C.   a majority of the members in the House of Commons
     D.   any government headed by a hereditary ruler, such as a king or queen

4.   What are the names of five political parties in Canada? _____

     _____

     _____

5.   What is another name for the lower house in the Canadian Parliament?
     A.   Liberal Party   B.   House of Commons
     C.   Senate   D.   New Democratic Party

6.   A prime minister is the leader of:
     A.   the political party that has a minority of members in the House of Commons
     B.   the political party that has a majority of members in the House of Commons
     C.   the political party that is appointed by the Queen of England
     D.   the political party that has a minority of members in the Senate

7.   Canada's Parliament meets in their capital city of _____.

8.   What are the two components of the Canadian cabinet? _____

     _____

Total Problems:	Total Correct:	Score:

Read the passage and answer the questions on the following page.

Wilton N. "Wilt" Chamberlain

A large and powerful man at 7'1", Wilt Chamberlain was considered by many to be the greatest offensive player in basketball history. Wilt's arrival into the league revolutionized the center position. His 100-point game against the New York Knicks on March 2, 1962, is an incredible record which will probably never be broken.

Wilt "The Stilt" Chamberlain was born in Philadelphia, Pennsylvania, on August 21, 1936. Coming out of high school, Wilt was a highly regarded player and had his choice of universities. He decided to attend the University of Kansas, where he led the Jayhawks to the 1957 NCAA tournament finals.

After leaving the University of Kansas, he briefly toured with the Harlem Globetrotters before joining the Philadelphia Warriors in 1959. He made an immediate impact there, winning both the Rookie of the Year and the MVP awards in his first season. He averaged an amazing 38 points and 27 rebounds per game. He went on to win a championship with the Philadelphia 76ers in 1967.

In 1968, Chamberlain went to the Los Angeles Lakers, where he teamed up with Jerry West to bring a championship to Los Angeles. This was a very talented Lakers team, but their championship hopes were constantly thwarted by the Boston Celtics. However, in 1972 Wilt and the Lakers won the championship. During this season, the Lakers set an NBA record, winning 33 straight games. Much of Chamberlain's early dominance was due to his tremendous size. But, during the later battles with the Celtics, Chamberlain showed he also possessed athleticism, speed, and unmatched basketball skills.

After fourteen seasons in the NBA, Chamberlain retired as a member of the Lakers in 1973. During his career, he won seven scoring titles, two NBA titles, and was named MVP of the league on four separate occasions. He is one of only two players to ever score over 30,000 points. On October 11, 1999, Chamberlain died of an apparent heart attack in California.

Read each question. Circle the letter beside the correct answer.

1. In which city was Wilt Chamberlain born?
    A. Los Angeles
    C. Philadelphia
    B. Kansas City
    D. New York

2. Which event occurred first?
    A. The Lakers set an NBA record, winning 33 straight games.
    B. Coming out of high school, Wilt was a highly regarded player.
    C. He won both the Rookie of the Year and the MVP award.
    D. He won seven scoring titles and two NBA titles.

3. In what year did Chamberlain retire from the Lakers?
    A. 1973
    C. 1999
    B. 1972
    D. 1959

4. With which of the following teams did Chamberlain not play?
    A. Jayhawks
    C. Lakers
    B. Atlanta Hawks
    D. Harlem Globetrotters

5. Against which team did Chamberlain score 100 points?
    A. Philadelphia Warriors
    B. Los Angeles Lakers
    C. Harlem Globetrotters
    D. New York Knicks

6. How tall was Wilt Chamberlain?
    A. 1'7"
    C. 7'1"
    B. 71"
    D. 117"

7. Before joining the Philadelphia Warriors, Wilt briefly toured with the:
    A. Philadelphia Warriors
    B. Los Angeles Lakers
    C. Harlem Globetrotters
    D. New York Knicks

8. What is another word for "thwarted" as used in the fourth paragraph: ". . . but their championship hopes were constantly thwarted by the Boston Celtics."
    A. confirmed
    C. opposed
    B. started
    D. encouraged

Total Problems:	Total Correct:	Score:

49

Read the passage and answer the questions on the following page.

Oceania: Islands of the Pacific

Oceania is a name used to refer to the widely scattered islands of the central and south Pacific; Australia and New Zealand are frequently included. Virtually all the islands are volcanic peaks built upon submerged volcanic bases.

Australia is the world's smallest continent, and it is also the oldest. It is about the same size as the United States, not including Alaska. The small continent of Australia is like an enormous island, with 23,000 miles of coastline. There are no volcanoes or rugged new mountains on the continent.

Another island found in Oceania is New Zealand which has everything from mountains and waterfalls to seashores and hot springs. New Zealand has two main islands, North Island and South Island. South Island is larger than North Island and has a major mountain range, the Southern Alps.

The islands of Oceania can be sorted into three main groups. The name of each group tells something about its islands.

Polynesia means "many islands," but the name makes most people think of a warm, sunny climate, palm trees, and sandy beaches. Polynesia includes Tahiti, American Samoa, and, far to the east, Easter Island. Hawaii, the western-most state of the United States, is located within the area of Polynesia. Polynesia is spread over a huge stretch of ocean, which covers about 15 million square miles. The isolation of the islands in this area, as well as their small size, have limited their economic development.

You can probably guess the size of the islands of Micronesia from the name. Micronesia means "tiny islands." Micronesia contains more than 2,000 islands. Most of these islands are atolls (a coral island or string of coral islands and reefs forming a ring that nearly encloses a lagoon).

Melanesia means "black islands," a name given to the islands possibly because of the dark vegetation of their hillsides. Melanesia lies south of the equator, west of Polynesia, and northeast of Australia. Fiji and the Solomon Islands are part of Melanesia. Papua New Guinea, the eastern half of the island of New Guinea, is the largest country in Melanesia. It has a rugged, mountainous terrain. Heavy rainfall in the mountains collects in streams that cross swamps and forests.

Answer the following questions. Write your answers in the spaces provided.

1. Oceania can be sorted into three main groups: _____

   _____

2. In addition to the three main groups, _____ and _____
   are frequently included in Oceania.

3. Micronesia, which means, "_____ ,"
   contains more than 2,000 islands, most of which are atolls.

4. _____, which lies south of the Equator, is a name given to
   the islands possibly because of the dark vegetation of their hillsides.

5. _____, the world's smallest continent, is about the size of
   the United States, not including Alaska.

6. Another island found in Oceania is _____, which has
   everything from mountains and waterfalls to seashores and hot springs.

7. Covering about 15 million square miles, _____ includes
   Tahiti, American Samoa, and Easter Island.

8. _____ are coral islands and reefs forming a ring that nearly
   encloses a lagoon.

9. Name three of the islands that make up Melanesia: _____

   _____

| Total Problems: | Total Correct: | Score: |

Read the passage and answer the questions on the following page.

Marilyn Monroe

Marilyn Monroe, a popular female entertainer during the 1950s, was born on June 1, 1926 in Los Angeles. Her father, Edward Mortensen, and her mother, Gladys Baker, were unable to care for the little girl known as Norma Jean Baker. She spent most of her childhood in foster homes and orphanages.

Later in her life, she found work as a model. With her ambition to become an actress, Marilyn studied at the Actors Studio in New York City. During her acting career, she starred in such hits as *Niagara*, *Gentlemen Prefer Blondes*, and *How to Marry a Millionaire*. Even though she was busy as a model and actress, she still found time to marry three husbands.

Her first marriage of four years was to a seaman named James Daugherty. Her second marriage of nine months was to the major-league baseball player Joe DiMaggio. Her third marriage of almost five years was to the American playwright Arthur Miller.

Marilyn Monroe died in Los Angeles on August 5, 1962 from an overdose of sleeping pills. Her death was shocking and traumatic for the whole world. Even though Miss Monroe has been dead for over thirty-eight years, she is still considered an American icon by some people.

On October 27-28, 1999, the famous auction house Christie's of New York held one of its most famous auctions. The title of the auction was "The Personal Property of Marilyn Monroe." Sales for both days totaled over $13 million dollars. The highlight of the sale was the "Happy Birthday" dress that Marilyn wore at Madison Square Garden on May 19, 1962, to sing to President John F. Kennedy. The long white dress sold for $1,276,000 to "Gotta Have It," a collectibles gallery in New York.

Some other highlights of the famous Christie's auction included Marilyn's diamond and platinum eternity band that Joe DiMaggio gave her after their wedding in 1954. The ring was sold to an anonymous bidder for $772,500. Her baby grand piano sold for $662,000 and a Mexican cardigan sold for $167,500. Tommy Hilfiger, a famous contemporary designer, purchased three pairs of denim blue jeans for $42,550, worn by Marilyn in 1954 in the movie *River of No Return*.

Tony Curtis, a movie star who co-starred with Marilyn in *Some Like It Hot*, said in attending the auction that Marilyn would be "moved and stunned" that people "still love her."

Read each question. Circle the letter beside the correct answer.

1. At the Christie's auction, Marilyn Monroe's famous "Happy Birthday" dress sold for:
    A. $772,500   B. $662,000
    C. $13,000,000   D. $1,276,000

2. Sales for both days at Christie's auction for the personal property of Marilyn totaled over:
    A. $13,000,000   B. $1,276,000
    C. $772,500   D. $662,000

3. To whom did Marilyn sing "Happy Birthday" at Madison Square Garden?
    A. President John F. Kennedy   B. Joe DiMaggio
    C. Arthur Miller   D. Tommy Hilfiger

4. Who gave Marilyn the ring that sold for $772,000.00?
    A. Tommy Hilfiger   B. Joe DiMaggio
    C. Arthur Miller   D. President John F. Kennedy

5. Which one of the following is not a hit movie in which Marilyn starred?
    A. *Sands of the Desert*   B. *How to Marry a Millionaire*
    C. *Gentlemen Prefer Blondes*   D. *Niagara*

6. Marilyn Monroe spent most of her young life in:
    A. Hollywood   B. orphanages and foster homes
    C. New York City   D. Mexico

7. Another word that means the same as "icon," in the fourth paragraph, is:
    A. beauty   B. actress
    C. idol   D. friend

8. Who bought Marilyn's blue jeans at the Christie's auction?
    A. President John F. Kennedy   B. Joe DiMaggio
    C. Tony Curtis   D. Tommy Hilfiger

9. What was the reason for Monroe's death in 1962?
    A. car accident   B. accidental drowning
    C. overdose of sleeping pills   D. filming accident

Total Problems:	Total Correct:	Score:

Read the passage and answer the questions on the following page.

Puerto Rico: A State?

Puerto Rico has been a self-governing commonwealth since 1952. As a commonwealth, Puerto Rico is a possession of the United States, but it is governed by its own constitution. Citizens of Puerto Rico have many of the rights and responsibilities of United States citizens; however, Puerto Ricans do not have the right to vote in national elections, and they are not required to pay federal taxes.

Some people in Puerto Rico are not satisfied with its status as a commonwealth. They want Puerto Rico to become a state of the United States. The movement to make Puerto Rico a state has gained wide support during recent years. Supporters believe that political, social, and economic conditions in Puerto Rico would improve if statehood were acquired. With statehood, Puerto Rico would be directly represented in the United States Senate and the House of Representatives. Federal funds would become available to provide housing and jobs for people who are unemployed there.

Baltasar Corrada del Rio, a former mayor of San Juan, explained that statehood would provide Puerto Rico with local self-government, as well as more political participation in Washington, D.C. As a state, Puerto Rico would continue to elect its own governor, as well as senators and representatives to its legislature. In addition, Puerto Ricans would be afforded equal participation in the United States Senate, fair representation in the House of Representatives, and a share in the responsibility to pay federal taxes. The island would also continue to have its two flags and its two anthems.

However, other Puerto Ricans believe that the island should remain a commonwealth. They feel that becoming part of the United States might cause them to lose their language and their culture. They believe that commonwealth status lets them keep and protect their Hispanic culture. They feel that if Puerto Rico becomes a state, Congress might impose English as their official language, an action which would lead to a lessening of the island's Hispanic culture. Among those who oppose the idea of Puerto Rican statehood are citizens who prefer to maintain the status quo and those who favor independence. The three main political parties in Puerto Rico reflect the preferences for statehood, status quo, and independence.

Miquel A. Herandez Agosto, former president of the Puerto Rican Senate, explained that Puerto Ricans are a Spanish-speaking people who cherish their Hispanic culture and would not exchange it for any material benefits. They are also proud of their linkage with the United States, but are not willing to relinquish Spanish as their first language nor to change their Hispanic culture for the "American way of life."

Read each question. Circle the letter beside the correct answer.

1. What is the main issue of this passage?
    A. whether Puerto Rico should become a state or remain a possession of the United States
    B. whether Puerto Rico should pay federal taxes
    C. whether Puerto Rico should continue to have two flags and two anthems
    D. whether Puerto Rico should change its official language

2. What is the view of those Puerto Ricans in favor of statehood?
    A. Statehood would mean Puerto Rico would lose its language.
    B. Statehood would mean Puerto Rico would lose its culture.
    C. Statehood would mean losing their status quo.
    D. Statehood would improve the political, social, and economic conditions in Puerto Rico.

3. What is the position of those Puerto Ricans who oppose statehood?
    A. Puerto Ricans would be afforded equal participation in the United States Senate.
    B. Becoming part of the United States could cause Puerto Rico to lose its language and culture.
    C. Puerto Ricans would be available for federal housing and jobs.
    D. Puerto Rico would continue to have its two flags and its two anthems.

4. Puerto Rico has been a self-governing commonwealth since:
    A. 1950   B. 1952
    C. 1956   D. 1958

5. If Puerto Rico were to become a state, it would continue to elect its own:
    A. governor   B. prime minister
    C. president   D. king

6. If Puerto Rico were to become a state, some Puerto Ricans believe that English might be imposed as their official language by the United States:
    A. the Senate   B. Congress
    C. the House of Representatives   D. Parliament

7. In the fourth paragraph, "status quo" means:
    A. a state   B. unpopular
    C. a number   D. existing state of affairs

Total Problems:	Total Correct:	Score:

55

Read the passage and answer the questions on the following page.

Hurricanes: Natural Disasters

A hurricane is a powerful, swirling storm that begins over a warm sea. When a hurricane hits land, it can cause great damage through fierce winds, torrential rain, flooding, and huge waves crashing ashore. A powerful hurricane can destroy more property than any other natural disaster.

The winds of a hurricane swirl around a calm central zone called the eye, which is surrounded by a band of tall, dark clouds called the eye wall. The eye is usually about 10 to 20 miles in diameter and is free of rain and large clouds. In the eye wall, large changes in pressure create the hurricane's strongest winds. These winds can reach 200 miles per hour. Damaging winds may extend 250 miles from the eye.

Hurricanes are referred to by different labels, depending on where they occur. They are called *hurricanes* when they happen over the North Atlantic Ocean, the Caribbean Sea, the Gulf of Mexico, or the Northeast Pacific Ocean. Such storms are known as *typhoons* if they occur in the Northwest Pacific Ocean. Near Australia and in the Indian Ocean, they are referred to as *tropical cyclones*.

Hurricanes are most common during the summer and early fall. In the Atlantic and the Northeast Pacific oceans, for example, August and September are the peak hurricane months. Typhoons occur throughout the year in the Northwest Pacific but are most frequent in summer. In the North Indian Ocean, tropical cyclones strike in May and November. In the South Indian Ocean, the South Pacific Ocean, and off the coast of Australia, the hurricane seasons run from December to March. Approximately 85 hurricanes, typhoons, and tropical cyclones occur each year throughout the world.

Read each question. Circle the letter beside the correct answer.

1. What word refers to the calm, central zone which is surrounded by a band of tall, dark clouds?
   A. eye
   B. eye wall
   C. hurricane
   D. cyclone

2. Which one of the following statements is false?
   A. Hurricanes occur over the North Atlantic Ocean.
   B. Typhoons are frequent in the summer.
   C. Hurricanes are common during the early fall.
   D. Hurricanes occur over the Northwest Pacific Ocean.

3. What are the peak hurricane months in the Atlantic and Northeast Pacific areas?
   A. August, October   B. September, November
   C. August, September   D. June, July

4. Winds in hurricanes can reach speeds up to:
   A. 250 miles per hour
   B. 200 miles per hour
   C. 20 miles per hour
   D. 85 miles per hour

5. A hurricane begins:
   A. when it hits land
   B. with a cool front
   C. over a warm sea
   D. with thunder and lightning

6. A hurricane is called a hurricane when it happens over all but one of the following areas:
   A. Caribbean Sea   B. Northwest Pacific Ocean
   C. Gulf of Mexico   D. Northeast Pacific ocean

7. Damage from a hurricane may extend how far from the eye?
   A. 85 miles   B. 250 miles
   C. 20 miles   D. 200 miles

8. Approximately how many hurricanes, typhoons, and tropical cyclones occur each year?
   A. 200   B. 85
   C. 250   D. 20

Total Problems:	Total Correct:	Score:

57

Read the passage and answer the questions that follow. Circle the letter beside each correct answer.

Spain: Dictatorship to Democracy

In 1975 Spain emerged from a long dictatorship to become a peaceful, democratic country. That year, Prince Juan Carlos became king of Spain. He took over after the death of Francisco Franco, who had ruled the country as a dictator.

Spain's government is somewhat different from the governments of other southern European countries. Although Spain is governed by an elected parliament, it also has a monarch. In this respect, Spain's government is like that of Great Britain.

Under Franco's rule, free elections and political parties had not been allowed in the country. When Juan Carlos came to power, the government of Spain was completely changed. First, the Spanish people elected a new parliament. Then, a new constitution was both written and approved in 1978. It established a parliamentary democracy with King Juan Carlos as head of the government.

Under the new constitution, the legislative branch—called the *Cortes*—is divided into two houses. Most of the power is in the lower house, called the Congress of Deputies, which is made up of 350 members elected by the people. The upper house is called the Senate.

1. Spain's government is similar to Great Britain's because both governments have a:
   A. dictatorship   B.   Senate
   C. president   D.   monarch

2. In what year did dictatorship end in Spain?
   A. 1979   B.   1972
   C. 1975   D.   350 A.D.

3. The first thing the Spanish people did after Carlos came to power was:
   A. elect a new parliament   B.   build a new palace
   C. execute Franco   D.   repeal the income tax

4. What two things were not allowed in the country under Franco's rule?
   A. free elections, private businesses   B.   free elections, political parties
   C. political parties, private businesses   D.   political parties, visiting dignitaries

5. What was the name of the Spanish dictator?
   A. Juan Carlos   B.   King Cortes
   C. Francisco Franco   D.   Great Britain

| Total Problems: | Total Correct: | Score: |

Name _____

Refer to the recipe to answer the questions at the bottom of the page. Circle the letter beside each correct answer.

Making Chicken Gumbo Soup

Ingredients

    1 stewing chicken
    1 cup flour
    1/4 cup bacon drippings
    4 cups boiling water
    2 cups skinned, seeded tomatoes
    1/2 cup fresh corn, cut from the cob
    1 cup sliced okra
    1 large green pepper—seeds and membrane removed, or 2 small red peppers
    1/2 teaspoon salt
    1/4 cup diced onion
    1/4 cup uncooked rice
    5 cups water

Directions

Cut the chicken into pieces and sprinkle with flour. Brown the meat in the bacon drippings. Pour the boiling water over the browned meat. Simmer, uncovered, until the meat falls from the bones. Strain the stock and reserve. Debone and chop the meat. Place the chopped meat and the stock in a soup kettle with the vegetables, rice, and additional water. Simmer, uncovered, about 30 minutes or until the vegetables are tender. Season to taste. Makes about 12 cups.

1. What is an appropriate substitution for the large green pepper?
    A. 1 cucumber   B. 2 small red peppers
    C. 2 squash   D. 3 chili peppers

2. How long do you simmer the meat after it has been chopped and placed in the soup kettle?
    A. 5 minutes   B. 12 minutes
    C. 30 minutes   D. 35 minutes

3. What is the first thing to do in making the soup?
    A. Cut the chicken into pieces and sprinkle with flour.
    B. Sprinkle the chicken gumbo with flour.
    C. Add 1/4 cup bacon drippings to 4 cups of hot water.
    D. Boil 4 cups of water and add flour.

4. After the ingredients have cooked, approximately how many cups of soup will this make?
    A. 2 cups   B. 5 cups
    C. 4 cups   D. 12 cups

Total Problems: Total Correct: Score: **59**

Read the experiment. Circle the letter beside the correct answer.

Growing Bread Mold

Problem:
Do hidden variables affect the results of
an experiment?

Materials:
slice of bread
2 jars with lids
medicine dropper

Procedure:
1. Tear a slice of bread in half.
2. Place each half into a separate jar.
3. Use the medicine dropper to moisten each half with 10 drops of water. Cover the jars.
4. Place one jar in sunlight and the other jar in a dark closet.
5. Observe the jars every few days for about two weeks. Record your observations in a
   data table. Once the experiment is completed, what conclusion can you draw?

Observations:
1. Did you observe mold growth in either jar?
2. If so, describe any differences or similarities in mold growth in the two jars.
3. Do you think that light affects the growth of bread mold? If so, how?

1. Which necessary ingredient is not listed in the materials list?
   A. mold
   B. water
   C. test tube
   D. foil

2. According to the directions, one jar should be placed in a dark closet and the other jar
   placed in:
   A. the kitchen   B. the science lab
   C. a drawer of a desk   D. the sunlight

3. If you follow the directions, the first thing to do is:
   A. Gather all the materials together on the kitchen counter or in the science lab.
   B. Place 10 drops of water on each piece of bread.
   C. Tear a slice of bread in half.
   D. Fill each jar with 2 cups of water.

Total Problems:	Total Correct:	Score:

Name _____

Refer to the recipe to answer the questions at the bottom of the page. Circle the letter beside each correct answer.

Let's Make Caramel Cream Fudge

Ingredients

1 cup brown sugar	2 tablespoons butter
1 cup sugar	1 teaspoon vanilla
$\frac{1}{8}$ teaspoon salt	1 cup broken black walnuts
$\frac{1}{3}$ cup corn syrup	2 teaspoons oil
1 cup milk	

Directions

(1) Place sugars, salt, corn syrup, and milk in a large, heavy pan. (2) Cook these ingredients quickly, stirring constantly until they boil. (3) Cook and stir 3 minutes. (4) Reduce the heat and cook until the mixture reaches the softball stage—230°. (5) Place the butter in the bottom of a mixing bowl. (6) Remove pan from heat and at once pour mixture over butter. Do not stir. (7) When cool, add vanilla and beat until creamy. (8) Just as the mixture loses its gloss, stir in the walnuts. Pour onto an oiled cutting board. (9) Cut into squares when set and store tightly covered.

1. After the ingredients have reached the boiling point, how many minutes should you cook and stir them?
    A.   2 minutes
    B.   3 minutes
    C.   4 minutes
    D.   5 minutes

2. What is the first thing you do in the directions?
    A.   Cook all of the ingredients quickly, stirring them constantly.
    B.   Place butter in the bottom of a mixing bowl or use an electric mixer.
    C.   Put the ingredients in a large, heavy pan.
    D.   Remove pan from heat and at once pour mixture over butter.

3. What ingredient is added in step 7?
    A.   1 teaspoon vanilla
    B.   1 cup broken black walnuts
    C.   2 tablespoons butter
    D.   1 cup brown sugar

4. After you have poured the mixture onto an oiled cutting board, what should you do next?
    A.   Just as the mixture loses it gloss, stir in 1 cup broken black walnuts.
    B.   Cut into squares when set and store tightly covered.
    C.   When cool, add 1 teaspoon vanilla.
    D.   Remove the lid, reduce the heat, and cook until mixture reaches a softball stage.

Total Problems: _____   Total Correct: _____   Score: _____   **61**

Name _____

Matter In Ocean Water

Read the experiment. Circle the letter beside the correct answer.

Matter In Ocean Water

Problem:
Do you know from where some kinds of matter in ocean water come?

Materials:
You will need some clean sand, a jar with a screw top, two milk cartons, a large needle, and some table salt. You will also need a teaspoon, two paper cups, four blocks of wood, a measuring cup, and some water.

Procedure:
1. Wash the sand by putting it into the jar with clean water. Then, screw the top on so that it fits well and shake the jar several times.
2. Let the jar stand for a few minutes, and carefully pour off only the water. Wash the sand in this way two more times so that the sand will be very clean.

3. Cut the top off each milk carton. With the large needle, make five or six holes in the bottom of each carton.
4. Add washed sand to each carton until it is about two-thirds full. Then, mix a teaspoon of table salt with the sand in one of the cartons. Now, place both cartons on wooden blocks over the cups.
5. Pour 50 ml of water into each carton. Let the water flow through the sand into each cup.

Observations:
1. Will the water in both cups look the same?
2. Where do you think some of the matter in ocean water comes from?

1. After placing the sand into a jar with clean water, you then:
   A. Let the jar stand for a few minutes.
   B. Wash the sand several times and let stand.
   C. Clean the sand, using the two milk cartons and table salt.
   D. Screw the top and shake the jar.

2. All of the following materials are needed except:
   A. two milk cartons and two paper cups   B.   a ruler and a tablespoon
   C. a measuring cup and water   D.   sand and a large needle

3. The last procedure is:
   A. to let the jar stand for a few minutes and pour off only the water
   B. to pour 50 ml of water into each carton
   C. to mix a teaspoon of table salt with the sand in one of the cartons
   D. to make five or six holes in the bottom of each carton

62

| Total Problems: | Total Correct: | Score: |

© Carson-Dellosa CD-2205

Read the recipe and answer the questions that follow. Circle the letter beside the correct answer.

Making Banana Pudding

Ingredients
> 1 cup sugar (separated into $3/4$ and $1/4$ cup)
> $1/3$ cup all-purpose flour
> $1/4$ teaspoon salt
> 2 cups milk, scalded
> 2 eggs, separated
> 1 teaspoon vanilla extract
> 25 vanilla wafers
> 4 bananas, sliced

Directions
(1) Combine $3/4$ cup sugar, flour, and salt in top of double boiler. Mix well and stir in milk. (2) Cook about 15 minutes, stirring constantly. (3) Beat the egg yolks until thick and lemon-colored. (4) Gradually stir one-fourth of the hot mixture into the yolks; add remaining hot mixture, stirring constantly. (5) Cook 2 minutes longer. Remove from heat and add vanilla. Cool. (6) Line a 1-quart baking dish with half of the vanilla wafers. Next, add a layer of sliced bananas. (7) Top with half of the pudding. Repeat layers. (8) Beat egg whites until soft peaks form. Then gradually add $1/4$ cup sugar and beat until stiff. Spread meringue over the pudding and bake at 350° for 15 minutes. Servings: 6

1. All the following are false for step 5, except one:
    A. Cook 1 minute longer.
    B. Remove from heat and add wafers.
    C. Cool.
    D. Line a 1-quart baking dish with half of the bananas.

2. In which step do you add a layer of bananas?
    A. step 7   B. step 8
    C. step 5   D. step 6

3. Which of the following statements is true for step 1?
    A. Combine flour, salt, and eggs in top of double boiler.
    B. Combine salt, flour, and sugar in top of double boiler.
    C. Combine $1/2$ cup sugar, flour, and milk in top of double boiler.
    D. Combine flour, salt, and vanilla in top of double boiler.

Read the poem and answer the questions that follow. Circle the letter beside the correct answer.

A Carpet's Point of View

Mine is a humble existence;
I'm here to cover the floor.
Occasionally, I get vacuumed,
and I ask for nothing more.

Parties are what I really hate,
getting trampled and worn.
So many spills and so much wear,
I look shabby and forlorn.

Time has passed and now I'm old.
Soon, I will be replaced,
but I've collected memories,
and those cannot be erased.

Winter was my favorite season,
when children would lie down, warm and snug.
They'd brush my fur with their tiny hands,
and I felt like more than a rug.

Mine is a humble existence though;
I'm just here to cover the floor.
I've served my purpose with comfort and love,
and could ask for nothing more.

1.   Winter was the carpet's favorite season because:
    A.   Children would lie on it and make it feel like a rug.
    B.   Children would lie on it and make it feel like more than a rug.
    C.   Children would lie on it and spill drinks on it.
    D.   They would vacuum it and make it feel worn.

2.   The carpet appears to be human throughout the poem in all except one of the following examples:
    A.   ... and I felt like more than a rug.
    B.   I ask for nothing more.
    C.   ... getting trampled and worn.
    D.   Mine is a humble existence.

| **Total Problems:**   **Total Correct:**   **Score:** |

Read the poem and answer the questions that follow. Circle the letter beside the correct answer.

The First Day of Spring

I look out the window to see the grass;
the grass is no longer the color of brass.
There are birds in the trees
and there are honeybees.

The first day of spring is here,
so that means that summer is near.
It is the day of the happy farmer,
because he knows the days will be warmer.

The days are long
like the birds' songs.
It is the first day of spring,
and the birds are ready to sing.

1. "The days are long/like the birds' songs." In this line the days are compared to songs. What is the writing technique when one thing is compared to another thing using the word "like"?
    A. metaphor   B. symbol
    C. pun   D. simile

2. Why is the farmer happy?
    A. because the grass is getting greener
    B. because the weather is getting warmer
    C. because he does not like the winter
    D. because he has a new tractor

3. When two words sound the same, as "grass" and "brass" do, this is called:
    A. rhythm   B. simile
    C. rhyme   D. poetry

4. "The First Day of Spring" contains:
    A. three lines   B. three stanzas
    C. twelve verses   D. twelve stanzas

Total Problems:	Total Correct:	Score:

Read the poem and answer the questions on the following page.

What Would We Do?

What would we do
without the light of the sun?
Where would we go,
and how would we get there?

What would we do
without the flowers and trees?
What would we see,
and what would we smell?

What would we do
without the rivers and streams?
How would we live,
and what would we taste?

What would we do
without the birds and the bees?
What would we hear,
and what would we sing?

What would we do
without the moon and the stars?
What would we dream,
and how would we feel?

What would we do
without the animals on earth?
Who would instruct us
and how would we know?

What would we do
without the heavens and earth?
To feed us and guide us
along nature's wonder of ways.

Read each question. Circle the letter beside the correct answer.

1. According to the poet, specifically, what do the heavens and earth do for us?
    A.   They help us to see and smell everything around us.
    B.   They feed us and guide us along nature's wonder of ways.
    C.   They help us to hear, sing, and taste everything around us.
    D.   They instruct us and make our dreams come true.

2. The poet believes that the moon and the stars provide humans with an opportunity to:
    A.   teach and think
    B.   hear and sing
    C.   dream and feel
    D.   see and smell

3. In the last stanza, another word for "heavens" would be:
    A.   God   B.   universe
    C.   stars   D.   planets

4. The poet believes that birds and bees provide humans with an opportunity to:
    A.   hear and sing   B.   dream and feel
    C.   see and smell   D.   teach and know

5. Every stanza has two questions, except stanza:
    A.   # 1   B.   # 5
    C.   # 3   D.   # 7

6. In stanza # 2, what senses are mentioned?
    A.   sight and hearing   B.   sight and smell
    C.   hearing and taste   D.   hearing and touch

7. Which one of the following statements could possibly be the main idea?
    A.   The light of the sun is something we couldn't live without.
    B.   Flowers, trees, birds, and bees are things we couldn't live without.
    C.   Nature is all around us, yet we don't seem to realize we couldn't live without it.
    D.   The animals teach us how to live each day of our lives.

8. A word that means the opposite of the word "wonder" in stanza # 7 is:
    A.   ordinary   B.   star
    C.   amazement   D.   think

Total Problems:	Total Correct:	Score:

Read the poem and answer the questions that follow. Circle the letter beside the correct answer.

Morning

The soldiers of the dawn
ride on the sun's rays.
Slowly they take the day
like a helpless pawn.
They bathe themselves
in the dew that cleanses
the Earth anew.
Retreating, they take
the light captive,
only to return it
the next day.

1. "The soldiers of the dawn/ride on the sun's rays." The soldiers are under the command of:
   A. the moon
   B. the general
   C. the sun
   D. the president

2. In line 1, the word "soldier" is a writing technique called:
   A. simile
   B. alliteration
   C. setting
   D. metaphor

3. Regarding "they bathe themselves," in line five: who is they?
   A. dew
   B. soldiers
   C. animals
   D. plants

4. What is the meaning of the word "retreating" in line eight?
   A. withdrawing
   B. forcing
   C. surrendering
   D. hearing

5. Which word rhymes with "dawn"?
   A. take
   B. rays
   C. pawn
   D. day

Total Problems: _____ Total Correct: _____ Score: _____

Read the poem and answer the questions that follow. Circle the letter beside the correct answer.

O Christmas Tree

It was the night before Christmas,
and the tree was sparkling like a diamond in the sun,
with ornaments glittering and glistening in the light,
while tiny bulbs, like a million jewels, were dancing everywhere.

Crowned by an angel, the tree was protected and guarded.
Looking at the tree, I was filled with unbelievable sensations.
Suddenly to my horror and dismay the angel toppled,
ornaments shattered like glass and little bulbs cracked like lightning.

Waiting for the light show to end, I gazed in disbelief,
as my kitty sat watching and looking at me
with huge yellow eyes and a big happy grin.
She had a look on her face that was worth a million.

Picking her up out of the muddle and leaving everything behind,
quickly darting off to bed,
I left my parents to recover and recollect,
as my kitty and I wait for Santa.

1. Paying attention to the context clues surrounding the word, choose another word that means the same as "muddle" in line 13.
   A. mud puddle   B. mess
   C. blood   D. water

2. What causes the Christmas tree to topple?
   A. a cat   B. the angel
   C. too many lights   D. Santa Claus

3. The tiny bulbs on the tree are compared to:
   A. an angel   B. a cat
   C. jewels   D. the sun

4. What is protecting and guarding the tree?
   A. lightning   B. angel
   C. kitty   D. poet

Read the poem and answer the questions that follow. Circle the letter beside the correct answer.

A Seat on a Bus

As I sat there
on the bus that day,
I was very tired
with not a whole lot to say.
You told me to get up,
and I did not know what to do.
You are a white man;
I'm supposed to listen to you.
I am tired of all the things they say
about the problems
in our nation today.
I saw the look you gave
when I wouldn't meet your demand.
But for a person like me
you'd never lend a hand.
I'm not disrespectful; I mean,
I'm not trying to be.
I am trying to make a point
that I hope you can see.
I didn't mean any trouble,
a fight, or a fuss.
And all of this happened
over a seat on a bus.

1. According to the poem, what did the speaker do when asked to "get up"?
   A. stood up   B. didn't get up
   C. started a fight   D. kept reading a newspaper

2. You can draw the conclusion that the speaker in the poem is:
   A. white   B. an old person
   C. black   D. a student

3. The main idea of the poem is:
   A. A white person should be able to sit anywhere on a bus.
   B. Fights and fusses can often erupt on a bus.
   C. Blacks and whites cannot get along on a bus.
   D. Any person, black or white, should be allowed to sit anywhere on a bus.

| Total Problems: | Total Correct: | Score: |

Refer to the graph to answer each question. Write each answer in the space provided.

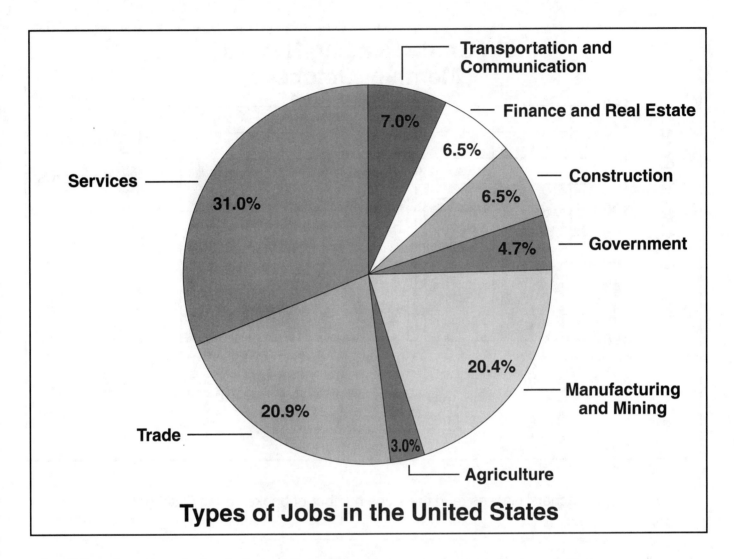

Types of Jobs in the United States

1. What does the whole circle graph represent? _____

2. What are the three largest categories of jobs found in the United States?

    A. _____ , B. _____ ,

    and C. _____ .

3. In which category are most workers employed? _____

4. Which area employs the smallest number of workers? _____

5. Approximately _____ % of the nation's workers have jobs in manufacturing and mining.

6. Finance and real estate employ _____ % of the nation's workers.

Total Problems:	Total Correct:	Score:

Refer to the graph to answer each question. Write each answer in the space provided.

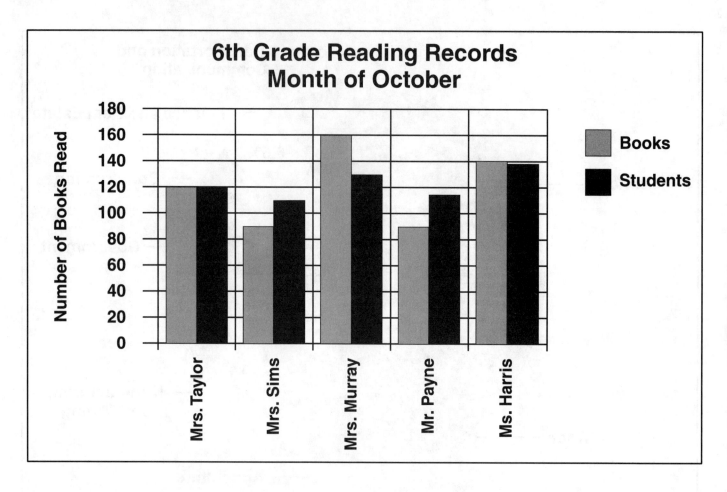

6th Grade Reading Records
Month of October

1. Which two teachers' classes read the same number of books during October?

    _____

2. Which sixth grade teacher's class read the most books during October? _____

3. How many more books did Mrs. Murray's class read than Ms. Harris's class? _____

4. During October, how many total books were read by Mrs. Taylor's, Mrs. Sims's, and

    Mr. Payne's classes? _____

5. Which teacher had the most students? _____

6. Which teacher had the least number of students in his or her class? _____

7. Which teacher had the highest percentage of books read based on the number of students?

    _____

72 | Total Problems: _____   Total Correct: _____   Score: _____ |

Refer to the graph to answer each question. Write each answer in the space provided.

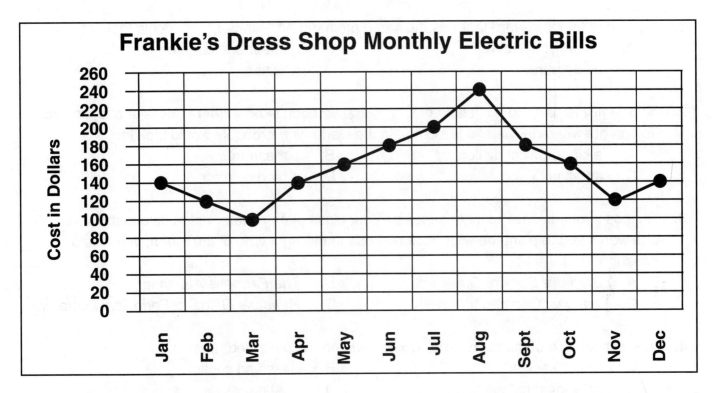

1. Which month had the highest cost in electricity? _____

   Why? _____

   _____

2. Which month had the lowest bill? _____ Why? _____

   _____

3. Which 3 months had the same electric bills? _____

4. If Frankie's Dress Shop was in Appleton, Wisconsin, instead of Atlanta, Georgia, how might

   the graph differ during August? _____

   _____

5. How might Frankie's Dress Shop use this graph for future planning? _____

   _____

6. Explain the fluctuations in the graph. _____

   _____

Total Problems:	Total Correct:	Score:

Read each question. Circle the letter beside the correct answer.

1. If you had to find a word that has the same meaning as "somber," you would look in:
   A. an encyclopedia
   B. a telephone directory
   C. a thesaurus
   D. an atlas

2. Your family is going to the island of Crete, and you don't know where this island is located. To find out where this island is located in the world, you probably would look in:
   A. a biographical dictionary
   B. a thesaurus
   C. an atlas
   D. a card catalog

3. Suppose your science teacher suggests your class plant a watermelon field in the spring. If she wants you to plant the watermelon seeds at the right time of the moon, you would consult:
   A. *Bartlett's Book of Quotations*
   B. *The Farmer's Almanac*
   C. *National Geographic Atlas*
   D. *Reader's Guide to Periodical Literature*

4. In which section of the newspaper would you find "help wanted" ads?
   A. sports section
   B. classified section
   C. entertainment section
   D. front page

5. Your English teacher asked you to find the meaning of "turbulence." You would look in:
   A. an atlas
   B. a thesaurus
   C. a dictionary
   D. an encyclopedia

6. You are doing research on the Biltmore Estate near Asheville, North Carolina. If you wanted general information on this famous house, you could look in:
   A. an encyclopedia
   B. *Reader's Guide to Periodical Literature*
   C. a thesaurus
   D. an international *Who's Who?*

7. In a book, where do you find the title, author, and publisher?
   A. index
   B. title page
   C. glossary
   D. table of contents

8. If your teacher asked you to bring in recent information on the president and one of his recent trips abroad, you would probably look in:
   A. an encyclopedia
   B. a card catalog
   C. a dictionary
   D. a newspaper

Total Problems: _____ Total Correct: _____ Score: _____

Refer to the dictionary entry to answer each question. Circle the letter beside the correct answer.

> **home**, (hom) n. 1. the place where a person lives; one's dwelling place. 2. the city, state, or country where one was born or reared. 3. a place where one likes to be; restful or congenial place. 4. one's final resting place; the grave. 5. the members of a family; household or the life around it. 6. an institution for orphans, the infirmed, aged, etc. 7. the natural environment, or habitat, of an animal, plant, etc. adj. 1. of one's home or country; domestic. 2. of, or at the center of operations: as, a home office. 3. to the point; effective. adv. 1. at, to, or in the direction of home. 2. to the point aimed at: as, *he drove the nail home*. 3. to the center or heart of a matter; closely.

1. What is the part of speech for the definition of "home" that means "at the center of operations"?
   - A.   adverb
   - B.   verb
   - C.   adjective
   - D.   noun

2. Which numbered definition means "the members of a family"?
   - A.   6
   - B.   5
   - C.   3
   - D.   2

3. What is definition # 7 for the word "home"?
   - A.   institution for orphans
   - B.   of one's home or country
   - C.   one's dwelling place
   - D.   natural environment of an animal

4. In which sentence below is the word "home" used as a noun?
   - A.   The corporate lawyer's home office is located in San Francisco.
   - B.   Jan ran home to see if she left her library books on the dining room table.
   - C.   Ian's home is situated between two rolling hills of green grass and heather.
   - D.   The home box office was closed when we were there at 4:00 this afternoon.

5. In which sentence below is the word "home" used as an adjective?
   - A.   I need to go home to check with my grandmother before I go to the movie.
   - B.   At halftime, the home team's score was tied with the opposing team's score.
   - C.   My dad left his new boots at home and couldn't climb the steep mountain.
   - D.   Grandma boarded the plane and said to the pilot, "Steer this plane home. I'm tired."

Total Problems: _____   Total Correct: _____   Score: _____

Refer to the sample card catalog entry to answer each question. Circle the letter beside the correct answer.

Title: *Buffalo Hunt*

Author: Freedman, Russell

Published: Holiday House,1988

Physical description: 52 pp.

Notes: Examines the importance of the buffalo in the lore and day-to-day life of the Indian tribes of the Great Plains and describes hunting methods and the uses found for each part of the animal that could not be eaten.

Notes: Interest grade level: 3-7

Subject: Nonfiction

Subject: Animals

1. According to the card catalog, what do we know about the book?
   A. The book is about the Great Plains Indians.
   B. This book is about the importance of buffalo to the Great Plains Indians.
   C. This book describes farming methods of the Great Plains Indians.
   D. This book describes stories told by the Great Plains Indians.

2. The person who wrote *Buffalo Hunt* is:
   A. Running Press
   B. Holiday House
   C. Great Plains
   D. Russell Freedman

3. How many pages does the book contain?
   A. 1988 pages
   B. 37 pages
   C. 52 pages
   D. 528 pages

4. For what grade level is the book intended?
   A. 2-4 grades
   B. 5-8 grades
   C. 1-9 grades
   D. 3-7 grades

5. What is the name of the publishing company?
   A. Holiday House
   B. Great Plains
   C. Running Press
   D. Russell Freedman

Total Problems: _____   Total Correct: _____   Score: _____

Refer to the sample entry from *Reader's Guide to Literature* to answer each question. Circle the letter beside the correct answer.

> Taming Maggie [separation anxiety in dogs] S. Schultz. il *U.S. News & World Report* v.126 no.8 p.62-4 Mr 1 '99

1. What is the name of the article in the entry above?
   A. "Separation Anxiety in Dogs"   B. "U.S. News & World Report"
   C. "Taming Maggie"   D. "S. Schultz"

2. Where is the article found, according to the entry above?
   A. S. Schultz   B. *U.S. News & World Report*
   C. Separation Anxiety in Dogs   D. Taming Maggie

3. In which month and year is the article found?
   A. May 1999   B. May 1962
   C. March 1999   D. March 1962

Refer to the sample title page entry to answer each question.

> **For the Love of Dogs**
>
> Kim Campbell Thornton
> Virginia Parker Guidry
>
> Publications International, Ltd.

4. Publications International, Ltd., is the name of the:
   A. author   B. publisher
   C. book   D. city

5. Who wrote the book?
   A. Kim Thornton
   B. Kim Thornton and Virginia Guidry
   C. Virginia Guidry
   D. Kenneth Thornton and Virginia Campbell

Refer to the sample index to answer each question. Circle the letter beside the correct answer.

INDEX

Fleas, 132,133

Fleming's classification of dogs,
   313, 314

Folding portable dog pens, 53

Follicles, 149

Food, See also Diet.

Food poisoning antidote, 142

Food substitutes for chewing, 32

Food supplements, 30

"Foot," as coursing term, 189

Foot care, 43

"Force" retrieving, 239

Foreign breeds, 331-337

   Australian Cattle Dog, 331

   Australian Kelpie, 331

   Bichon Frise, 330

   Chinook, 332

   Chinese Crested Dog, 332

   Catalan Sheepdog, 331

   Drentsche Partrijshond, 332

   Finnish Spitz, 333

   Istrian Pointer, 333

   Lurcher Dog, 333

   Marenna Sheepdog, 333

   Portuguese Pointer, 333

   Rumanian Sheepdog, 333

   Sealydale Terrier, 333

   Spinone Dog, 333

   Svensk-Valhund, 333

   Tibetan Mastiff, 334

   Wheaten Terrier, 335

Foreign travel, 56-61

Formula, See Milk.

Fossils of early dogs, 282, 283

1. Suppose you wanted to find information on the Rumanian Sheepdog. On what page would you look?
   A.   331
   B.   337
   C.   333
   D.   332

2. What is the main category or main heading found on pages 331-337?
   A.   Catalan Sheepdog
   B.   Australian Cattle Dog
   C.   Foreign Breeds
   D.   Australian Kelpie

3. Beside the category "Food," there is a statement "See also Diet." This is called a cross reference. This means that:
   A.   One can also find information on food by looking under the main category "Diet."
   B.   One can only find information on food by looking under "Food."
   C.   There is no available information on food under the category "Food."
   D.   There is no information available on food under "Food" or "Diet."

4. If your dog chews the furniture in your house and you wanted to find information on chewing, you could look on what page?
   A.   142
   B.   32
   C.   332
   D.   not available

Total Problems: Total Correct: Score:

Name _____ Following Directions

Read the passage and answer the questions. Circle the letter beside the correct answer.

Peanut Butter Cookies

Ingredients
1 cup flour
½ tsp baking soda
⅛ tsp salt
¼ cup butter
2 cups peanut butter
½ cup brown sugar
1 egg
½ cup milk
⅛ tsp vanilla
chopped and salted peanuts
1 cup granulated sugar

Directions
1. Preheat the oven to 375°F.
2. Stir together flour, soda, and salt and set aside.
3. Beat butter and peanut butter together for 30 seconds.
4. Add sugars to butter and peanut butter mixture and beat until light and fluffy. Add egg, milk, and vanilla. Beat well.
5. Add dry ingredients to mixture and beat until well blended. Stir in peanuts.
6. Shape dough into one-inch balls, and roll balls in additional sugar. Place on an ungreased cookie sheet. Press the dough balls with a fork to form a crisscross pattern.
7. Bake for 10 minutes.

1. How long should you beat the butter and peanut butter together?
   A. 10 minutes (B) 30 seconds C. 375 minutes D. 10 seconds
2. What step comes immediately after adding the vanilla, milk, and egg?
   (A) beat well B. stir in sugar C. bake 10 minutes D. preheat oven
3. What is the first thing you do in the baking directions?
   A. Shape dough into one-inch balls. B. Beat butter and peanut butter together.
   C. Bake for 10 minutes. (D) Preheat the oven to 375°F.
4. What ingredients are added in step number 4?
   (A) vanilla, sugars, milk, egg B. vanilla, peanuts, milk, egg
   C. sugars, flour, vanilla, egg D. milk, peanuts, egg, vanilla
5. These directions demonstrate how to:
   A. make a peanut butter sandwich B. make chocolate chip cookies
   (C) make peanut butter cookies D. make vanilla cookies

© Carson-Dellosa CD-2205 Total Problems: Total Correct: Score: **9**

Name _____ Finding the Main Idea

Read each passage. Circle the letter beside each correct answer.

Spencer
Because the four brothers are exceptionally talented, Spencer is the band that I admire the most. All four brothers have amazing singing voices, and since they are brothers, their voices blend together beautifully. In addition to being vocally gifted, the brothers also write all of their music and play their own instruments. I find Spencer's song lyrics to be unique, and the music very uplifting. Consequently, the guys have been showered with much-deserved success. Another factor that emphasizes the talent of the Spencer quartet is the brothers' ages—none of the four are even old enough to vote. To be able to sing well, write songs, and play music are three things that I believe contribute to true musical talent.

1. The main idea of the paragraph is:
   (A) The writer is impressed with Spencer's singing ability.
   B. The writer is surprised that the Spencers are not old enough to vote.
   C. The writer would like to meet Spencer.
   D. The writer is disappointed that the Spencers don't play their own instruments.

Mormons
In 1846, the Mormon migration to the Great Salt Lake area began. Approximately 12,000 Mormons made the historic journey, the largest single migration in American history. They founded a community in the midst of the desert called Deseret. Later the Mormons changed the name to Salt Lake City.

2. The main idea of the paragraph is:
   A. about the Mormon Tabernacle in Salt Lake City
   B. a description of the desert in southwestern United States
   (C) about the Mormon migration to Salt Lake City
   D. that the Mormons suffered great losses in their migration of 1846

10 Total Problems: Total Correct: Score: © Carson-Dellosa CD-2205

Name _____ Finding the Main Idea

Read each passage. Circle the letter beside each correct answer.

Plants
After seeds are formed, they are usually scattered far from where they grew. The scattering of seeds is called seed dispersal. Seeds are dispersed in many ways. If you have ever picked a dandelion puff and blown away all its tiny seeds, then you have helped to scatter the seeds. Dandelion seeds, along with maple and certain pine seeds, are usually scattered by the wind. Maple seeds contain little wing-like structures which enable them to spin through the air like tiny propellers.

1. The main idea of the paragraph is:
   A. Dandelions are difficult to control on the lawn.
   (B) Seeds are dispersed in different ways.
   C. Seeds contain wing-like structures.
   D. Dandelions can be picked.

Presidential Election
In 1992, the Republicans supported President George Bush in his bid for reelection, while the Democrats nominated Arkansas Governor Bill Clinton as their candidate. The Independent third party chose billionaire Texas businessman H. Ross Perot as their candidate. During the campaign, Clinton pledged to reconstruct America's healthcare system and welfare system. He favored an active government that supported pro-business policies and stressed American's concerns about the economy. On the other hand, Ross Perot urged the need to end the federal government's deficit spending—spending more money than it takes in. In the election, Clinton won with only 43% of the popular vote. Bush won 38% of the popular vote, and Perot received 19%, the best showing for a third-party candidate since 1912. Many voters felt that President Bush would win a second term in office, but a lengthening recession raised doubts about his leadership.

2. The main idea of the paragraph is:
   A. to reconstruct America's healthcare and welfare systems
   B. the presidential election of Ross Perot in 1992
   C. the reelection of President Bush in 1992
   (D) the presidential election of Bill Clinton in 1992

© Carson-Dellosa CD-2205 Total Problems: Total Correct: Score: **11**

Name _____ Arranging the Sequence

As you read the passage, pay attention to the clues that let you know the order in which events happened. Circle the letter beside each correct answer.

SCUBA
This summer my dad and I shared an experience that I will never forget. In the Gulf of Mexico, we went scuba diving. This adventure did not start out as I would have liked. I became seasick on the boat ride to the oil rig. Therefore, some of the crew members tried to persuade me not to go diving, but nothing was going to prevent me from this experience. I just decided to forget and have the best time of my life. Since my dad tends to breathe heavily, he became low on air after we had been down a short while. My dad had to surface, so the dive master and I decided to go up with him. Since we had a sufficient supply of air, we decided to continue our dive at twenty-five feet. I was concerned that staying at this shallow depth I would miss seeing the magnificent ocean life. To my surprise, however, this turned out to be the perfect place. Swimming around at this depth, I found myself surrounded by nurse sharks. I was amazed that they paid no attention to me, even as I gently touched them. I hated to call the perfect dive to a halt, but our air supply was running low. This day was extremely special because I shared it with my dad. This was the most unforgettable experience I have ever had.

1. Which event happened first?
   A. My dad had surfaced, so the dive master and I decided to go up with him.
   B. Swimming around at twenty-five feet, I was surrounded by nurse sharks.
   (C) On the boat ride to the oil rig, I became seasick.
   D. The nurse sharks paid no attention to me, even as I gently touched them.
2. What happened after the father's air became low?
   (A) The father had to resurface.
   B. The father decided to continue diving without the gear.
   C. Some of the crew members tried to persuade the writer not to dive.
   D. The writer decided to dive to fifty feet.
3. Which of the following events happened last?
   A. On the boat ride to the oil rig, the writer of this story became seasick.
   (B) The divers called it a day because their air supply was running low.
   C. The writer was surrounded by nurse sharks.
   D. The writer's dad resurfaced because of low air.

12 Total Problems: Total Correct: Score: © Carson-Dellosa CD-2205

79

© Carson-Dellosa CD-2205

Name _____   Arranging the Sequence

As you read the passage, pay attention to the clues that let you know the order in which events happened. Circle the letter beside each correct answer.

Dr. King

Martin Luther King, Jr., born on January 15, 1926 in Atlanta, Georgia, was the son and grandson of Baptist ministers. He was 19 years old when he graduated from Morehouse College, and three years later earned the bachelor of divinity degree at Crozer Theological Seminary. In 1954, before obtaining his Ph.D., King became the pastor at Dexter Avenue Baptist Church in Montgomery, Alabama. There he was president of the Montgomery Improvement Association, which organized the famous bus boycott. The next year he was awarded a Ph.D. at Boston University where he met his wife, Coretta Scott. Perhaps Dr. King's most famous speech, "I Have a Dream," was delivered to over 200,000 spectators in 1963 in Washington, D.C. For his extraordinary work in the civil rights movement, Dr. King was honored with the Nobel Peace Prize in 1964. He led many nonviolent marches and protests, trying to help African-Americans obtain the rights they deserved. Often he was mistreated and abused because he was a black man. In early 1968, he went to Washington, D.C., to deliver his "Poor People's Campaign." On April 4, 1968, on the balcony of the Lorraine Motel in Memphis, Tennessee, Dr. King was shot and killed by James Earl Ray.

1. Which event happened first?
   A. In 1964 Dr. King was honored with the Nobel Peace Prize.
   B. He delivered his famous speech, "I Have a Dream," in 1963.
   C. In Montgomery, Alabama, King was pastor at Dexter Avenue Baptist Church.
   D. King was nineteen years old when he graduated from Morehouse College.

2. What did King do after making his speech "I Have a Dream"?
   A. He became pastor of Dexter Avenue Baptist Church.
   B. He was assassinated in Memphis, Tennessee.
   C. He was honored with the Nobel Peace Prize.
   D. He was awarded a Ph.D. degree.

3. What happened 14 years after King became pastor of Dexter Avenue Baptist Church?
   A. He was shot and killed in Memphis, Tennessee.
   B. He was president of the Montgomery Improvement Association.
   C. He was awarded a Ph.D. at Boston University.
   D. He was honored with the Nobel Peace Prize.

© Carson-Dellosa CD-2205 | Total Problems: Total Correct: Score: | **13**

Name _____   Drawing Conclusions

As you read each passage, pay attention to clues that will help you to draw a conclusion about the information. Circle the letter beside each correct answer.

Cracker Garden

Mom can always get me to do extra chores by saying she will take me to the Cracker Garden. The smells of the deep, wooden floor, along with the signs of food on the wall intrigue my appetite as I approach the polyurethane-coated table. I sit to look at the variety of hot cuisine from which I have to choose. There are so many choices that it is difficult to decide what my preference is going to be on any certain day. Then, in an instant, I know what I crave. The usual treats for me consist of fresh chicken tenderloins, steamy green beans, creamy chicken and dumplings, and the absolute best caramel milk shake on the face of the earth. As I await the arrival of my meal, I sit and play the challenging pegboard game. My eyes light up as soon as I see the waitress coming with our food. To watch her walk all the way from the kitchen to our table seems to take an eternity. However, the wait is well worth it. I always walk away from the Cracker Garden with a smile on my face.

1. From the story one can conclude that:
   A. The child enjoys fresh turkey tenderloins.
   B. The child's mom can persuade the child to do extra chores by agreeing to take the child to the Cracker Garden.
   C. The child enjoys dartboard games.
   D. The mom enjoys the Cracker Garden.

Drum Major

To be the drum major of a band has always been a dream of mine. When I entered the tenth grade, my dream came true. I was named the drum major of the Middleton High School Band. I went to many camps to help prepare for that position. However, there was more to being a drum major than what I was taught. Being drum major was not just a job where I led the band onto the field, conducted the halftime show, and then led the band off the field. When I became the drum major, it was an opportunity to show my love for music. I not only led the band and conducted the halftime show, I challenged the band to feel the music in their hearts.

2. The writer suggests that:
   A. He or she can make everyone in the band love music.
   B. There is more to being a drum major than having technical ability.
   C. The only part of being a drum major is conducting the halftime show.
   D. He or she is underqualified to be drum major.

14 | Total Problems: Total Correct: Score: | © Carson-Dellosa CD-2205

Name _____   Drawing Conclusions

As you read the passage, pay attention to the clues that let you know the order in which events happened. Circle the letter beside the correct answer.

The Berlin Wall

For 28 years the Berlin Wall divided the city of Berlin and its people into two cities: East Berlin and West Berlin. Hundreds of people died trying to escape across the Wall to West Berlin. Guards with searchlights and machine guns were stationed along the Wall in its 300 towers. Some people who tried to escape hid under cars or in coffins, while others swam canals or scaled the Wall with grappling hooks. With the reunification of Germany in 1990, the Wall was destroyed. Today, only one section remains as a memorial to its history and the people who died in their attempts to escape.

1. From the paragraph, one can tell that:
   A. Berlin was a bustling, commercial city.
   B. The guards in the towers were lenient and sympathetic.
   C. West Berlin welcomed East Berlin when the wall was destroyed.
   D. Escape would have been difficult and dangerous.

Coral Reefs

Coral reefs are limestone structures containing the shells of animals. Reefs are found in the warmer parts of the Pacific Ocean and the Caribbean Sea. The organisms that build reefs need sunlight to make their hard limestone skeletons, and the organisms cannot survive in waters colder than 18°C. There are three types of coral reefs: fringing, atoll, and barrier. Fringing reefs are coral reefs that touch the shoreline of a volcanic island. Atoll reefs are coral islands consisting of a reef surrounding a lagoon. Barrier reefs are coral reefs that are separated from the shore by an area of shallow water called a lagoon. The largest barrier reef on earth is the Great Barrier Reef of Australia. It is about 2,300 kilometers long and ranges from 40 to 320 kilometers wide. The Great Barrier Reef is rich in many kinds of animal and plant life.

2. One can tell that:
   A. Reefs are formed and found in relatively shallow waters.
   B. Some reefs might be found in the North Atlantic Ocean.
   C. Organisms that build reefs can be found in deep waters.
   D. Coral reefs are the remains of plant life.

© Carson-Dellosa CD-2205 | Total Problems: Total Correct: Score: | **15**

Name _____   Recognizing Supporting Details

Read the biographical passage and answer the questions on the following page.

Alfred Hitchcock

Alfred Hitchcock, born in Leytonstone in East London, was the youngest son of William and Emma Whelan Hitchcock. At only sixteen years of age, he left home to study engineering and navigation at the University of London. Hitchcock soon developed an interest in art and studied it in the evenings. He always had an interest in cinema, and after Paramount opened a studio in London, he was hired as a title designer for silent films.

Hitchcock made his full directorial debut with *The Pleasure Garden* (1925) which would touch off a long and much lauded career. He was one of the most creative and innovative directors to ever come onto the scene. In *The Lodger*, Hitchcock broke all conventional rules of film reality. In *Blackmail* (1929), his first film with sound, he created "subjective sound." In the story, a woman stabs a young man. In a conversation with her neighbor the next morning, Hitchcock gradually distorted every word of the neighbor's speech except "knife" in order to show the person's anxiety and train of thought.

After the success of *The Lodger*, Hitchcock was on a roll. *Blackmail* was successful, but it was *The Man Who Knew Too Much* (1934) that actually brought Hitchcock his first commercial success. The film dealt with the investigation of a family, and the suspense and intrigue that lies within the most basic unit of society. This theme would occur throughout Hitchcock's work.

When Hitchcock moved to America, he was welcomed with open arms. His first film was *Rebecca* (1940). Most critics feel that *Shadow of a Doubt* (1943) was Hitchcock's best pre-World War II work. The film explored the values of American family life and uprooted some conventional beliefs. The plot line, about a young woman who suspects her visiting Uncle Charlie of being a murderer, is merely a go-between for more interesting themes.

There are four films which always stand apart when discussing Hitchcock: *Rear Window* (1954), *Vertigo* (1958), *North by Northwest* (1959), and *Psycho* (1960). These four films explore psychological disturbances—a topic of utmost interest to Hitchcock. Hitchcock continued to produce strong work through the 1960s. His most famous work of this period was *The Birds* (1963), and the most notorious was *Marnie* (1964)—an intriguing character study film. In the 1970s, he returned to England and finished his long career back where he had started. There he produced *Frenzy* (1972) and *Family Plot* (1972), which was his last film.

16   © Carson-Dellosa CD-2205

Page 17

Name _____   Recognizing Supporting Details

Read each question. Circle the letter beside each correct answer.

1. Which film brought Hitchcock his first commercial success?
   A. Blackmail   B. Rear Window
   C. The Lodger   (D) The Man Who Knew Too Much

2. What was Hitchcock's first film after coming to America?
   (A) Rebecca   B. The Pleasure Garden
   C. Shadow of a Doubt   D. The Birds

3. Where was Alfred Hitchcock born?
   A. America   (B) England
   C. Canada   D. France

4. As a young man, what was one of Hitchcock's first jobs?
   A. engineer   B. director
   (C) title designer for silent films   D. navigator

5. What was Hitchcock's most famous work of the 1960s?
   (A) The Birds   B. Marnie
   C. The Lodger   D. The Pleasure Garden

6. With which Hollywood studio did Hitchcock work?
   A. Disney   B. Universal
   C. Columbia   (D) Paramount

7. Which film distorted every word of a neighbor's speech except the word "knife"?
   A. The Birds   B. Marnie
   (C) Blackmail   D. The Lodger

8. In what decade did Hitchcock return to his homeland to finish his long career?
   (A) 1970s   B. 1960s
   C. 1950s   D. 1940s

9. Which film portrays a young woman who suspects her uncle of being a murderer?
   A. Rear Window   (B) Shadow of a Doubt
   C. Psycho   D. Frenzy

10. The Pleasure Garden is important because it launched Hitchcock's:
    (A) directorial debut   B. first commercial success
    C. most famous work   D. first film with sound

Total Problems: Total Correct: Score: **17**

© Carson-Dellosa CD-2205

Page 18

Name _____   Identifying Figurative Language

Read the poems and circle the letter beside each correct answer.

Perfect Love

Bright, dazzling sunlight
Fills the sky,
Glimmering upon the water.
Colors of gold, red, and
Majestic purple clothe the
Clouds with a garment of
Shimmering silk.
The sky darkens and
A gentle hush
Falls over the land.
The world, full of awe,
Silently watches as
The sun goes
Softly to sleep in
The blue blanket
Of the sea.

1. "The sun goes/Softly to sleep in/The blue blanket/Of the sea." What does the underlined expression mean?
   A. It is dark and time to go to sleep.
   (B) The sun is setting in the west.
   C. The sun is going behind a cloud.
   D. It is cloudy and rainy.

2. "Colors of gold, red, and/Majestic purple clothe the/Clouds with a garment of/Shimmering silk." The underlined words represent sounds that together are called:
   A. metaphors
   B. similes
   C. personification
   (D) alliteration

Lady of the Harbor

Just beyond the crowded streets
She stands tall and brave,
Clothed in robes of green,
Her hand lifted high above the harbor.
Though she says nothing,
She speaks a thousand words.

3. "Clothed in robes of green, ..." The underlined expression means:
   (A) weathered by time
   B. she is wearing a bath robe
   C. she is wearing green leaves
   D. she resembles a tree

4. "Though she says nothing,/She speaks a thousand words." This means:
   A. her vocal chords do not function
   B. she is constantly talking
   (C) the Statue of Liberty is a symbol
   D. she uses sign language

18   Total Problems: Total Correct: Score: © Carson-Dellosa CD-2205

Page 19

Name _____   Identifying Figurative Language

Read the passage and circle the letter beside each correct answer.

The Race

It was a cool summer morning. Wiping the fog from the windows to my outer world, I plunge into the sparkling, blue water. Diving deeper, I hear sounds like tinkling bells from far away. The rush of coolness around my face sends me into a dizzying whirlwind. Everything trickles from my mind. With control I thought had left me, I gather myself. I press on toward the mark that is burned into my mind's eye. Suddenly, the race is over. I pull the goggles from my face and stand in the shallow water. Winded but not spent, I climb out and gaze upon the living world once again.

1. The swimmer is pressing toward the goal that is "burned into my mind's eye." What does the quoted expression mean?
   A. a burning eye
   (B) very clear in the swimmer's mind
   C. cannot think very clearly
   D. blurred vision

2. "Diving deeper, I hear sounds like tinkling bells from far away." What form of figurative language is the underlined expression?
   A. metaphor
   B. personification
   C. symbol
   (D) simile

3. "Winded but not spent, I climb out and gaze upon the living world once again." The underlined expression means:
   (A) not totally out of breath
   B. totally out of breath
   C. out of money
   D. a windy day

4. "With control I thought had left me, I gather myself." The underlined expression means:
   A. to pick up pieces of clothing
   B. cannot control his or her thoughts
   (C) thoughts of control become clearer
   D. the swimmer becomes faint and dizzy

Total Problems: Total Correct: Score: **19**

© Carson-Dellosa CD-2205

Page 20

Name _____   Identifying Inferences

Read each passage and circle the letter beside the correct answer.

Plant Growth Experiment

Your teacher has given you the following instructions for an experiment on the growth of plants:

Gather information. Buy two identical plants and potting soil. Using the soil, pot the plants in two different containers. Place one of the plants in the sun and the other plant in a shaded area. After a few days, record the growth of the plants. Conduct this experiment for two weeks, recording your results about every two to three days. At the end of two weeks, you should notice a difference in the two plants.

1. The inference is:
   A. Place one of the plants in the shade and the other plant in the sun.
   B. Buy two identical plants and potting soil.
   (C) The plant in the shade will not grow as well as the plant in the sun.
   D. Use the same potting soil for both plants.

Plane Ride

Although the plane was very small, it could seat four passengers. Darren was excited to be able to take his friend Billy up in his dad's plane. Billy was even more excited. He had never been in an airplane before. Darren had flown many times with his dad. After he introduced Billy to his dad, they took off into the wild blue yonder. From the air, they saw their town, their houses, and their school. As they flew over Darren's house, his dad tipped one of the plane's wings, and Billy saw a woman in the yard waving up at the plane.

2. The inference is:
   (A) Tipping a wing is a way of greeting someone on the ground.
   B. The pilot almost lost control of the plane.
   C. Darren's dad was not a good pilot.
   D. Billy was afraid when the plane tilted.

20   Total Problems: Total Correct: Score: © Carson-Dellosa CD-2205

Name _____ Analyzing Passages

Read each passage and circle the letter beside the correct answer.

A Consumer in the Marketplace

What skills do you need as a consumer in the business world? As a consumer, you need to be able to interpret advertisements and product labels. You need to be able to read and understand drug prescription labels, directions, and warnings. When you go shopping, you need to be able to figure out the best buys. You need to know how to balance your checkbook, fill out forms, file job applications, and do your taxes. Every day these basic skills come into play, and that is why they are so important to successful living.

1. The main idea of the passage above is:
   A. Doing your taxes requires filling out forms.
   B. Basic skills are very important to successful living.
   C. You need to be able to read product labels.
   D. Balancing your checkbook can be easy if you know how.

2. A "consumer" is someone who is:
   A. a business person   B. an advertiser
   C. a shopper   D. a pharmacist

Hurricane Floyd

Hurricane Floyd, one of the strongest storms ever tracked in the Atlantic Ocean, landed on the shores of North Carolina on Thursday, September 16, 1999. Floyd's winds, once up to 155 mph, moved up the east coast at about 75 mph. Meteorologists were saying that Floyd was predicted to be the biggest storm ever, but at the last minute, Floyd lost its punch and was downgraded to a tropical storm. Hurricane Andrew ranks as one of the worst United States catastrophes in terms of insured losses.

3. Which of the following statements is true?
   A. Hurricane Floyd is the biggest storm ever, in terms of losses.
   B. Hurricane Floyd moved up the Pacific Coast at about 75 mph.
   C. Hurricane Andrew struck the shores of North Carolina on Thursday, September 16, 1999.
   D. Hurricane Floyd had winds up to 155 mph.

4. A "meteorologist" is someone who:
   A. travels the east coast   **B.** studies weather
   C. lives in North Carolina   D. creates hurricanes

© Carson-Dellosa CD-2205

| Total Problems: | Total Correct: | Score: | **21** |

Name _____ Analyzing Passages

Read each passage and circle the letter beside the correct answer.

What Is that Word?

Words are symbols of ideas and understanding. Children want to learn, so they listen to words, put things together in their minds, and come up with a meaning. For example, suppose you didn't know what the word "plek" meant. (Plek isn't a word though.) But suppose you heard people saying, "I have to catch a plek," and "The plek is due at the station at 8:10 tonight," or "The freight plek had over 100 cars as it passed my house." What would you think the word plek meant in each of these situations?

1. After reading the passage, you can infer that "plek" means:
   A. millionaire
   B. car salesman
   C. train
   D. doctor

School Is Fun

I love school. When the alarm goes off in the morning around 6:30, I get so excited. I jump out of bed, take a shower and dress, eat breakfast, brush my teeth and hair, and leave for school. Every day, I cannot wait for my classes to begin.

2. What is the main idea in the passage?
   A. The author loves math class especially.
   B. The author loves school.
   C. The author enjoys taking a shower before breakfast.
   D. The author always brushes her teeth after breakfast.

Stress

We think of stress as being a bad thing. Stress can be a good or a bad thing. It depends on how you perceive and handle the stressful situation. Having to give a speech in class can be a good or a bad stressor. It just depends on how you feel. Stress can actually make you feel good, for example, when you win a game or fly in an airplane.

3. What is the main idea of the passage?
   A. Stress is a bad thing, and we should work to prevent it.
   B. Stress cannot be avoided in our society.
   C. School causes too much stress on teenagers.
   D. Stress can be good or bad.

22

| Total Problems: | Total Correct: | Score: |

© Carson-Dellosa CD-2205

Name _____ Analyzing Passages

Read each passage and circle the letter beside the correct answer.

Symbols in a Dream

Some people think that symbolism is a major part of dreams. Symbols can be represented through color, people, animals, places, and even clothes. Some symbols can be hard to interpret because we do not observe them when we are awake. Everything we have heard, seen, thought, felt, and imagined can be represented by symbols in a dream. We may even have multiple dreams at night, with each one containing a different symbol.

1. The main idea is:
   A. Symbols can be represented through color and people.
   B. Symbolism is a major part of dreams.
   C. Some symbols can be difficult to interpret.
   D. Everything we have heard can be represented in a dream.

2. Which one of the following statements is true?
   A. Symbols can be represented through color, people, animals, plants, and clothes.
   B. Symbols can be represented through color, people, animals, places, and changes.
   C. Symbols can be represented through color, people, animals, places, and clothes.
   D. Symbols can be represented through color, places, annuals, people, and clothes.

Women in Veterinary Medicine

The field of veterinary medicine has become increasingly open to women. Once generally a man's profession, this field is now open to both sexes. In 1910, the first two women were granted veterinary degrees. Since then, women have grown in number, stature, and influence in veterinary medicine. In 1998, there were approximately 59,000 practicing veterinarians, 30% of whom were women. To create support for women in the veterinary field, the women started the AWV (Association of Women Veterinarians). The number of women veterinarians has grown at a rate of almost six times greater than that of men during the first half of this decade.

3. The main idea is:
   A. Two women were granted veterinary degrees in 1910.
   B. Female veterinarians have grown at a rate of almost six times than that of men.
   C. In 1998, there were around 59,000 practicing veterinarians.
   D. The field of veterinary medicine has become increasingly open to women.

© Carson-Dellosa CD-2205

| Total Problems: | Total Correct: | Score: | **23** |

Name _____ Analyzing Passages

Read each passage and circle the letter beside the correct answer.

First Mention of Christmas

The first mention of the celebration of Christmas occurred in 336 A.D. in an early Roman calendar which indicates December 25 as the day of observance. This date of the celebration was probably influenced by non-Christian celebrations and rituals performed long before Christ's birth in Bethlehem. Teutonic and Celtic tribes held November feasts called "Jiuleis" or "Giuli," which celebrated the end of the harvest season. In Roman times the "Saturnalia" was celebrated for a week in December, to honor Saturn, their harvest god.

1. What were the feasts called that celebrated the end of the harvest season?
   A. Julius   **B.** Jiuleis
   C. January   D. Jill

2. The first mention of Christmas dates back to:
   A. 25 A.D.   **B.** 336 A.D.
   C. 17 A.D.   D. 336 B.C.

Dog Dreams

Dreaming is not limited to one stage of sleep. In fact, it is not even limited to humans. All mammals, with a few exceptions, dream every night. That means that when your dog is whimpering in its sleep, it might be having a nightmare. Furthermore, dreams do not even have to be visual. Blind people can dream using sounds and their other senses.

3. If your dog is whimpering sometimes at night, it might mean that:
   A. Your dog is sick.
   B. Your dog is dreaming.
   C. Your dog is happy.
   D. Your dog is snoring.

4. Which one of the following statements is false?
   A. Dogs dream.
   B. Most mammals dream.
   C. Blind people do not dream.
   D. Dreams do not have to be visual.

24

| Total Problems: | Total Correct: | Score: |

© Carson-Dellosa CD-2205

Panel 1 (page 25)

Name _____ Analyzing Passages

Read each passage and circle the letter beside the correct answer.

Engineering

Tradition says that the term "engineer" came from the workers who designed and constructed engines of war and structural works that served military purposes. Leonardo da Vinci, best known for his painting of the *Mona Lisa*, was a talented engineer as well as an artist. His projects involved a special type of windmill, an automatic device for pumping a ship's hull dry, the construction of a bridge between Galata and Istanbul, or Constantinople, and the erection of a drawbridge in order to reach the Anatolian coast.

1. Which one of the following statements is false?
   A. Leonardo da Vinci engineered a special type of windmill.
   B. Leonardo da Vinci painted the *Mona Lisa.*
   C. Leonardo da Vinci designed a drawbridge for Atlanta, Georgia.
   D. Leonardo da Vinci designed a bridge between Galata and Instanbul.

2. The term "engineer," according to tradition, is related to:
   A. famous painters
   B. the military
   C. the Senate
   D. the ocean

Hinduism

Hinduism is a collection of several Indian religions. Hindus believe that humans exist in a realm of illusion, or false reality, called maya. It is in this realm that souls are believed to be reincarnated. Reincarnation refers to the belief that the soul can be reborn in different physical forms after death. Hindus believe that the soul can be reincarnated as a god, human, animal, vegetable, or even mineral.

3. Reincarnation refers to a Hindu religious belief that:
   A. The soul is dead in a different physical form after death.
   B. The soul is dead in the same physical form after death.
   C. The soul does not exist in a different physical form after death.
   D. The soul is reborn in a different physical form after death.

4. Hinduism is a major religion found predominantly in the country of:
   A. Hindu
   B. India
   C. Maya
   D. Reincarnation

© Carson-Dellosa CD-2205 | Total Problems: | Total Correct: | Score: | **25**

Panel 2 (page 26)

Name _____ Analyzing Passages

Read each passage and circle the letter beside the correct answer.

The First Amendment

The First Amendment to the United States Constitution clearly states that Congress does not have the right to and will not diminish the freedom of speech of the people of the United States. The amendment states: "Freedom of speech is the right to speak out publicly or privately." This right is exercised in newspapers, magazines, books, radio, television, and movies. Since the United States is democratic, or governed by the people, freedom of speech is required.

1. The First Amendment to the Constitution of the U.S. guarantees:
   A. freedom to vote
   B. freedom to have a gun
   C. freedom of speech
   D. freedom to own property

2. Another expression for "democratic" is:
   A. governed by a Senate
   B. ruled by a prime minister
   C. ruled by a dictator
   D. governed by the people

Hypnosis

Hypnosis is a state that resembles sleep. It is induced by a person whose suggestions are readily accepted by the subject. Some hypnotherapists define it as an increased state of relaxation. In fact, the word comes from *Hypnos*, the Greek god of sleep. Some physicians use this technique to analyze a patient's problems and place suggestions into the patient's mind.

3. The main idea is that hypnosis is:
   A. a suggestive state that some doctors use to treat patients
   B. a way to relax and sleep better
   C. a way to get in touch with one's feelings
   D. a way to get in touch with one's next door neighbor

4. Hypnosis is a word derived from *Hypnos*, which refers to the:
   A. Greek god of sleep
   B. Greek god of conscience
   C. Greek god of mind
   D. Greek god of hippos

26 | Total Problems: | Total Correct: | Score: | © Carson-Dellosa CD-2205

Panel 3 (page 27)

Name _____ Analyzing Passages

Read each passage and circle the letter beside the correct answer.

Churchill Downs Racetrack

The Churchill Downs Racetrack contains 147 acres, but the actual track is one-mile long and eighty feet wide. The racetrack accommodations include 1,404 stalls for horses and seating for 48,500 people. Located in Louisville, Kentucky, the Churchill Downs Racetrack hosts the biggest horse race of the year—The Kentucky Derby. The derby is held annually on the first Saturday in May. The prize for first place is one million dollars. The fastest time ever recorded in the Kentucky Derby is one minute, 59 and two-fifths seconds. This is also the only time under two minutes.

1. Which one of the following statements is false?
   A. The prize for the winner is one million dollars.
   B. The racetrack can seat 48,500 people.
   C. The derby is held annually on the first Saturday in April.
   D. The fastest time recorded to date is one minute, 59 and two-fifths seconds.

2. How many horse stalls are located at the racetrack?
   A. 48,500
   B. 147
   C. 80
   D. 1,404

San Francisco

San Francisco, a beautiful city in California, contains some of the most historical monuments in America. Located there is one of the harshest prisons ever operated—Alcatraz. One of the most famous art museums in the United States, the Palace of the Legion of Honor, is also located in San Francisco. Other well-known symbols of the city are the Golden Gate Bridge and Golden Gate Park. San Francisco is also the home of the 49ers as well as the famous baseball team, the Giants. San Francisco has been described as a shimmering bay of steep, curving hills, wooden Victorian houses, and open green spaces.

3. What important historical monument in San Francisco was once a prison?
   A. Golden Gate Bridge
   B. Palace of the Legion of Honor
   C. Alcatraz
   D. Golden Gate Park

4. The name of the famous baseball team in San Francisco is:
   A. the Giants
   B. the Jets
   C. the 49ers
   D. the Braves

© Carson-Dellosa CD-2205 | Total Problems: | Total Correct: | Score: | **27**

Panel 4 (page 28)

Name _____ Where Is Grandpa?

Read the passage and answer the questions on the following page.

Where Is Grandpa?

Aunt Molly walked into the kitchen and saw Meg sitting at the table with a cup of coffee. "Billy was staring out the window again," Aunt Molly stated absentmindedly while pouring herself a cup of coffee.

"I know," Meg replied wearily. "I saw him when I passed his bedroom. I peeked my head in and tried to get him come down to breakfast. It was as if he didn't hear me. I just wish I knew what he was thinking. I feel so helpless. He is my son, and I am supposed to help him, but I don't know what to do."

Aunt Molly stood up and walked over, placing a comforting hand on Meg's shoulder. She said, "You know what the doctor said. The only thing we can do is be patient."

"I just wish I knew what he was thinking," said Meg.

"He probably feels to blame for his grandfather's accident," responded Aunt Molly.

Meanwhile, Billy stared out of the window into the beautiful morning. The air was a little cool this morning with a salty hint in the air. The waves were lapping the beach in rhythmic patterns. He thought of the last fishing trip with Grandpa. When Grandpa arrived that day, Billy had been waiting for hours. He and his grandfather always had great times fishing together, and he loved him very much. At the boat dock, their boat was easy to spot because it was the oldest one there. It needed a new paint job, but other than that, it was in great condition. They had a favorite fishing spot, and when they stopped, Billy threw the anchor into the water.

They caught a lot of fish, and early in the day the weather was beautiful. That afternoon however, dark clouds began to form on the horizon. Grandpa told Billy to raise the anchor so they could get home quickly. Billy hesitated and tried to convince Grandpa to fish just a little longer. Billy wished he had cooperated sooner, because after just a few minutes, the boat began to rock and waves came crashing over the side. Billy had just raised the anchor when he heard a loud splash. The next thing Billy could remember was waking up in his bed at home. Billy was sorry he hadn't listened to his grandfather sooner, and he hoped his grandfather would recover quickly from the accident.

A knock at his bedroom door brought Billy's thoughts away from the memory. As the door opened, Billy heard a familiar voice say, "Hey buddy, they say the fish are biting out there. Let's go!"

28 | © Carson-Dellosa CD-2205

Name _____   Where Is Grandpa?

Read each question and circle the letter beside the correct answer.

1. An inference one can make is that:
   A. Grandpa has recovered and is ready to go fishing again.
   B. Aunt Molly and Meg are worried about Billy.
   C. The weather was beautiful on the morning of their fishing trip.
   D. Billy's mother is angry at him.

2. The word "cooperate," in the seventh paragraph, means:
   A. go fishing
   B. listen
   C. dive into the water
   D. argue

3. The doctor told Aunt Molly and Meg to:
   A. give Billy fluids
   B. be patient
   C. call Billy's friends
   D. take Billy fishing

4. After reading the seventh paragraph, one can draw the conclusion that:
   A. Grandpa was knocked overboard by the crashing waves.
   B. Billy dropped the anchor into the water.
   C. A large fish had jumped out of, and back into, the water.
   D. The boat flipped over and dumped everyone into the water.

5. How does Billy cope with the boating accident?
   A. He visits Grandpa every day in the hospital.
   B. He discusses with Aunt Molly what happened.
   C. He has blocked the accident from his mind.
   D. He gets up every morning and has breakfast just as he normally would.

6. How was the weather the day of the accident?
   A. It was a beautiful afternoon.
   B. There was a storm in the morning.
   C. It was a beautiful day.
   D. There was a storm in the afternoon.

7. What is Billy doing as the story opens?
   A. visiting Grandpa
   B. staring out the window
   C. eating breakfast
   D. getting prepared to fish

© Carson-Dellosa CD-2205 | Total Problems: | Total Correct: | Score: | **29**

Name _____   Why Dolphins Jump Out of the Water

Read the passage and answer the questions on the following page.

Why Dolphins Jump Out of the Water

A long time ago on a bright afternoon, Sunny was feeling very sad. Moony asked, "What is wrong with you today, Sunny?"

Sunny replied, "I am tired of doing the same thing every day. I want an adventure."

To this Moony said, "I know a place that is very dark and needs sunshine."

"Where?" Sunny responded.

"The ocean," said Moony.

The next day Sunny said good-bye to all of his heavenly friends and fell from the sky with a big splash. Creating such a huge disturbance caused the animals in the sea to avoid Sunny. The animals swam away as quickly as possible, making Sunny very sad. What was Sunny going to do?

Toby, a brave dolphin, decided to investigate the disturbance and the intruder. After a lengthy conversation with Sunny, Toby learned that Sunny was nice and just wanted to be friends with everyone. Without waiting too long, Toby called all the fish and other dolphins together to meet Sunny.

The animals loved Sunny and spent hours playing together in their new lighted underworld. At first, everyone was excited to have light in their world under the ocean. But Bob, the king of the ocean, noticed after a few days that some of the plants and animals had actually begun to die. Sunny did not know why, but Bob did. Bob explained that many plants and animals in the ocean are accustomed to cold temperatures and no light. Now that Sunny was there, the temperature was warmer and there was much light.

Bob decided he would have to ask Sunny to leave. Sunny loved his new life and friends in the ocean and did not want to leave. Finally, Bob said, "Sunny, if you don't leave, the ocean will die. We do love you very much, but we can't survive if you stay."

After a minute, Sunny said, "Bob, I will leave, but may I stay one more night to say good-bye to all my friends?" Bob agreed that Sunny could stay one more night.

The next day, after saying a tearful good-bye to everyone, Sunny left. Before Sunny left, however, Toby told his new friend that he would never forget him. As a reminder of their friendship, Toby said he would occasionally jump out of the water into the light to say "hi" to Sunny in the sky.

With tears in his eyes, Sunny returned home to find Moony waiting and watching. Moony wanted to know everything about the trip into the ocean and all the friends Sunny had made. Furthermore, Moony said one day he might have to travel into the ocean to meet all of Sunny's friends. In the meantime, sometimes during the day or night, Moony can see a dolphin jumping out of the ocean with Sunny looking on and smiling.

30   © Carson-Dellosa CD-2205

Name _____   Why Dolphins Jump Out of the Water

Answer the questions below. Circle the letter beside the correct answer where appropriate.

1. Arrange the sentences in chronological order, from 1 to 6.

   __3__ Toby called all the fish and dolphins together.

   __1__ Sunny wanted an adventure.

   __4__ Bob decided to ask Sunny to leave.

   __6__ Moony can see a dolphin jumping out of the ocean.

   __2__ All the animals swam away as quickly as possible.

   __5__ Toby said he would occasionally jump out of the water.

2. Who was the "king of the ocean"?
   A. Toby
   B. Bob
   C. Sunny
   D. Moony

3. The names Sunny and Moony represent the sun and the moon. Therefore, the names are:
   A. similes
   B. metaphors
   C. symbols
   D. alliterative

4. Why did Sunny want to visit the ocean?
   A. He wanted to fish.
   B. He wanted a drink of water.
   C. He didn't want any friends.
   D. He wanted an adventure.

5. What can you infer from reading the story?
   A. Moony liked it when Sunny was away.
   B. Sunny does not belong in the sky; instead, Sunny belongs in the ocean.
   C. Bob, the king of the ocean, was mean to Sunny by asking Sunny to leave.
   D. Animals in the ocean cannot adapt to new, contrasting conditions without any problems.

6. The main idea of this story is:
   A. Some plants in the ocean need light to grow.
   B. Sunny wanted to make friends with all the people on earth.
   C. Everything has its role or function in the world.
   D. Dolphins, on occasion, jump out of the water.

© Carson-Dellosa CD-2205 | Total Problems: | Total Correct: | Score: | **31**

Name _____   Soccer Star

Read the passage and answer the questions on the following page.

Soccer Star

Once upon a time, in a small town in South Dakota, there lived a small boy. This little boy's name was Gunther. Gunther was different from all the other kids at his school because he was so much smaller than everyone else. At the primary and elementary schools, he was taunted and teased by the other kids because he was shorter and skinnier.

When Gunther went to the middle school, he found that the students were the same to him there as they were at the other schools; however, as the school year progressed, he began to grow little by little. Before his sixth grade year was over, he was almost as tall as the other kids in his class. No one hardly ever made fun of him anymore.

Then, soccer tryouts came around in the spring, and Gunther decided he would try out for the team. All the bigger boys that had been on the team before just laughed at him and began to make fun of him again. This naturally pushed Gunther to try harder to show the coach just what he could do. After a few weeks of running and working out, Gunther was in good condition.

During the first soccer game, the star player twisted his ankle, and the coach had to put Gunther in the game. None of the other players thought he would do well. On the first play, Gunther captured the ball and kicked a goal. The crowd cheered wildly for him. As Gunther ran down the field, the other players blocked for him and were amazed at his speed and agility. Finally, Gunther made the winning goal, and his teammates carried him off the field.

Gunther was cheered by the fans and his teammates after the game. For once in his life, he felt special. From that moment on, he was never made fun of again. He was considered a hero for being the player who scored the winning goal in the game against his school's arch rival.

32   © Carson-Dellosa CD-2205

Name _____ Soccer Star

Read each question and circle the letter beside the correct answer.

1. The main idea of the story is:
   A. Soccer is a fun sport for all young boys.
   (B) One should never give up, regardless of size and stature.
   C. One should always fight back.
   D. School can be a great place for learning new ideas.

2. Another word or expression that means the same as "agility" is:
   A. helpless
   B. angry
   C. slow
   (D) ability to move quickly

3. Which event occurred last in the story?
   A. He was taunted and teased by the other kids.
   (B) He was never made fun of again.
   C. Gunther decided he would try out for the team.
   D. He found that the students were the same to him there.

4. What conclusion can you draw from the story?
   (A) If one tries and never gives up, things will work out for the best.
   B. If one is short, then eating a lot of food will help one to grow taller.
   C. Soccer is more fun to play than football.
   D. Sixth grade is more challenging than any other grade.

5. Why was Gunther taunted and teased by the students?
   A. He was from a foreign country.
   B. He was an A student.
   (C) He was shorter than most children his age.
   D. His family was poor.

6. What mishap occurred that enabled Gunther to play in the first game?
   A. The star player was involved in a car accident on his way to the game.
   B. The star player slipped and fell in the locker room.
   C. The star player was suspended because of poor grades.
   (D) The star player twisted his ankle.

© Carson-Dellosa CD-2205 | Total Problems: | Total Correct: | Score: | **33**

Name _____ A Cow Tale

Read the passage and answer the questions on the following page.

A Cow Tale

Once upon a time, in a pasture far, far away there was a very disgruntled dairy cow. Clarabel was forced to work as a milk producer and was given very little time to enjoy even the little things in her life. She envied the other cows that just sat around all day eating and sleeping without a care in the world, or so she thought. If only she could change pastures, her life would greatly improve, but it seemed impossible. You see, Clarabel was a black and white spotted cow while the other cows were all brown with white faces. There was no way she could go against this obvious show of shameful bigotry. She had to come up with a plan.

Early one morning, it began to rain very hard in the pasture. Unfortunately, Clarabel was very thirsty and would have to walk to the other side of the pasture to get to the pond. She believed the rainwater to be impure and was sure it would lessen her spots. As she was approaching the water, she became weary because of the slippery grass. Then it happened; she slipped and fell into a huge, mud puddle. Horrified, she just lay there until after the rain had ceased. When she stood up, she was covered in mud from head to toe, completely brown except for a small spot on her face. At first, she was going to take a running leap into the pond to wash off the mud. Then it came to her—she looked like one of the cows from the next pasture.

Immediately, Clarabel had to get the attention of one of the neighboring ranchers. She moved as close as possible to the next pasture and began mooing as loudly as she could. This prompted one of the ranchers to come over to the fence. As he screamed and hollered something about "cow thieves" and "police," she was quickly led out of the fence and into the pasture she had been wanting to join for so long. She began trying to make friends with her new pasture pals. Clarabel had always had a very easy time making friends, but these cows seemed to have something on their minds. At nightfall, they all huddled in a circle in the center of the pasture and began to sing sad moo songs, while gently swaying back and forth. They kept saying something about "the burden of beef" and "fast food will be the end of us all." None of this made any sense to Clarabel, and it seemed that everyone was too occupied with these threats to explain them to her. Confused, Clarabel decided to go to sleep and worry about it in the morning.

When Clarabel awoke the next morning, she noticed all her fellow cows were being herded into big trucks and taken away. She was an intelligent cow and had managed somehow to learn to read a little. The trucks had words written on them about beef and hamburger. She was not familiar with either of these words and strained her ears to listen to the other cows. They were yelling at her saying, "run while you can" and "save yourself." It became apparent that for whatever reason these cows would not be returning.

Although she began running away, Clarabel soon ended up on a separate, smaller truck. Clarabel realized her truck was going toward her old pasture, the opposite direction from the others. When she arrived, she literally ran off the ramp and into her beloved pasture. Somehow she had been recognized and saved. As she walked up to the pond, she saw her reflection. All the mud was gone; it must have rained during the night. From that point on, Clarabel was glad to be a dairy cow and danced and mooed every time it rained.

34 | © Carson-Dellosa CD-2205

Name _____ A Cow Tale

Read the questions below. Circle the letter beside the correct answer where appropriate.

1. Arrange the sentences in chronological order, from 1 to 6.

   _4_ They all huddled in a circle in the center of the pasture and began to sing.

   _6_ She literally ran off the ramp and into her beloved pasture.

   _2_ Then it happened; she slipped and fell into a huge mud puddle.

   _5_ They were yelling at her, saying, "run while you can" and "save yourself."

   _1_ If only she could change pastures, her life would greatly improve.

   _3_ She moved as close as possible to the next pasture and began mooing.

2. The main idea of the story is:
   A. Cows should be allowed to enjoy themselves.
   (B) You should be satisfied with what you have.
   C. Dairy cows lead a hard life.
   D. A cow is just like a human.

3. In the last paragraph, Clarabel "walked up to the pond" and ". . . she saw her reflection." What inference can you make concerning why Clarabel was not taken on the trucks with the other cows?
   A. Clarabel was a cow with special privileges.
   B. The trucks were full and had no more room for Clarabel.
   C. The farmer did not want to get rid of Clarabel.
   (D) Only brown cows with white faces were taken away in trucks.

4. Choose the expression below which portrays "bigotry."
   A. placing two cows of the same breed into two different pastures with equal portions
   (B) giving special privileges to a cow who is brown and white, not black and white
   C. recognizing that one cow is bigger than another cow
   D. placing two cows in one pasture and three cows in another pasture

© Carson-Dellosa CD-2205 | Total Problems: | Total Correct: | Score: | **35**

Name _____ Pieces of Life

Read the passage and answer the questions that follow. Circle the letter beside each correct answer.

Pieces of Life

Thinking of her daughter as a child again, an old woman sits in her chair with her quilting supplies beside her. She places her wrinkled hand into a woven basket where many different colorful pieces of clothes lay. She reaches to the bottom to find her most precious possession. As she brings it into her lap, a tear gently runs down her wrinkled face. As she holds her double-ringed quilt in her trembling hands, memories of each piece begin to fill her with emotions. She glides her hands over each piece, as if she were remembering each minute of her life. Now she must piece together a new quilt because her youngest daughter will soon be married. Not only does this particular double-ringed quilt represent the unity of a man and woman, but it also represents a summary of her daughter's life.

Picking up the first piece of a dress, she remembers the day her little girl wore this home from the hospital. As each piece brings more memories, the old mother bonds them together, using the threads of life. These threads connect each day within the daughter's life. As she sews the pieces of different garments together, she knows that her daughter will do this one day. The tradition of making quilts will continue because it represents her job of helping to piece memories of her children's lives together.

1. In the second paragraph, what does the expression "threads of life" mean?
   (A) the way the old woman and her children's lives and the quilt are intertwined
   B. the way her daughter has spent her life
   C. memories of how she and her husband spent their lives
   D. represents all the spools of thread she has purchased

2. What evidence supports the expression in the first line "an old woman"?
   A. has several children
   B. making a quilt
   (C) wrinkled hands and face
   D. she reminisces

3. In the last line, ". . . to piece her children's lives together" means:
   A. The old woman is sewing pieces of quilt patterns together.
   (B) The old woman is sewing memories of her family into the quilt.
   C. The old woman is using a photo album to recall her children's lives.
   D. The old woman is trying to understand her children's behavior.

36 | Total Problems: | Total Correct: | Score: | © Carson-Dellosa CD-2205

Name _____ Woolby

Read the passage and answer the questions that follow. Circle the letter beside each correct answer.

Woolby

It was quiet. The sun had already gone down over the horizon, and a big, beautiful harvest moon could be seen. It was still mostly dark, though. All I could see were the shadowy outlines of the objects around me, and any movement would let them know I was there. I had my mission, and there was nothing that was going to keep me from completing it.

I decided to lay low and not make any move until just before 9:00. I had to go about 200 yards across the field in front of me to get to where I needed to be. I looked up and could see many bright lights. That was my goal, and I knew that getting there was going to be difficult.

I could tell that soon it was going to be closing time. I decided that I would have to make my move in a few minutes. Suddenly, acting on instinct, I leapt forward and began to run to the glimmers of light in the distance. I was sprinting across the open area at full speed weaving and dodging the enemy left and right. Children were counting on me, and I was not going to let them down.

Reaching the doorway of the building, inside where I wanted to be, I quickly made my way. Inside, I continued to run as I went down a long narrow aisle with all kinds of things on shelves on each side. I was sure the personnel were watching me, I was sure, but I had to make it to the package before I was led outside. As I turned the aisle, I saw it lying there. I grabbed it and ran in the direction from which I had come.

As I reached my destination and placed the package on the counter, she looked at me and then said, "Sir, would you like to pay cash, or charge your Woolby?"

1. Possibly, in what kind of store is the narrator?
   A. grocery store　　　　　　B. clothing store
   (C) toy store　　　　　　　　D. travel agency

2. The "personnel" in the fourth paragraph could be:
   A. teachers　　　　　　　　B. doctors
   C. the sixth grade class　　(D) sales clerks

3. "Charge your Woolby" means:
   A. Place a stamp on it.　　(B) Pay for the Woolby with a charge card.
   C. Attack the Woolby.　　　D. Change its looks.

4. In the first paragraph, the narrator states, "I had my mission." What is the mission?
   A. to enter the store before closing time and return a Woolby
   B. to enter the store before closing time and attack a Woolby
   (C) to enter the store before closing time and purchase a Woolby
   D. to enter the store before closing time and steal a Woolby

© Carson-Dellosa CD-2205　　| Total Problems: ___ Total Correct: ___ Score: ___ |　**37**

Name _____ Nails

Read the passage and answer the questions on the following page.

Nails

Once upon a time there was a very small, but unusual kitten named Nails. He was the smallest of the litter, but that did not seem to bother him at all. Nails was unusual because he was the only cat around that had such long nails, almost twice the length of most cats' nails.

One day, he and his family decided to take a short journey to town to visit Nails' Uncle Bob. Laughing and playing, everyone was having a swell time along the way, including Nails who stopped to chase a butterfly that had attracted his attention. However, this distraction caused Nails to fall well behind his family, who continued on the way to town and Uncle Bob's house.

After finally catching the big black and yellow butterfly, Nails realized his family had left him behind, probably not realizing he wasn't with them. "Oh no! How am I going to find my family?" he exclaimed to the butterfly, whose name was Billy.

"I can help you find your family if you will let me go," said Billy, after noticing that Nails was almost in a state of panic. Nails agreed and the two were off in hopes of finding the family.

Of course, this was no ordinary butterfly. He was quite intelligent, as intelligent as Albert Einstein, and he certainly knew his way around. Billy was very observant, too. He couldn't help but notice Nails' strange paws with the long nails. These nails were unlike any he had ever seen before. Billy couldn't resist asking, "Why are your nails so long? I've never seen any that long."

Nails replied, "I really do not know, but my mom has always told me they will come in handy one day." So Nails and Billy continued their search, with Billy directing the way. Soon, they came to a stream that had flooded its banks. Cats, of course, hate to get wet, so at the first sight of water, Nails stopped dead in his tracks. Billy asked, "What is wrong with you, little buddy?"

"Don't you know that cats hate water?" Nails responded in a voice that seemed angry and scared. Understanding Nails' fear now, Billy looked up and down the stream. He hoped he could find a very narrow stretch in the stream where they could cross. After looking for a short time, he didn't find a narrow stretch, but he did find a long tree that had fallen across the stream. "This will make a good bridge, and we can cross here," Billy said to Nails, who was waiting and watching.

Gathering his courage, Nails finally started across the crude bridge. He had gone about eight feet when he slipped. Billy yelled from above him, "Nails, are you all right?"

"I think so, but I can't do this. I want to back up," said Nails, again with disgust and fright in his voice. By this time, Nails was very scared and almost in tears.

Knowing this tree bridge was the only way to cross the stream, Billy said, "Use your long nails to hold onto the tree and go slowly across the log. It is the only way for you to find your family. You can do it, so trust yourself." Hesitating, Nails held his breath as he held on tightly to the log and began to creep across it. Slowly, he crawled to the other side, with Billy above, directing and encouraging him.

38　　© Carson-Dellosa CD-2205

Name _____ Nails

Read each question. Circle the letter beside the correct answer.

1. The main idea of the short story is:
   A. Long toenails are good things to have.
   B. Don't chase butterflies alone in the woods.
   (C) Never give up and rely on your inner strength as well as your physical strength.
   D. Don't talk with strangers if your parents aren't around.

2. Where was Nails going when he suddenly became lost and disoriented?
   A. to get groceries　　　(B) to visit Uncle Bob in town
   C. to find Billy　　　　　D. to play in the stream

3. What was the first question Billy asked Nails after their initial meeting?
   A. I can help you find your family if you will let me go.
   B. How am I going to find my family?
   C. What is wrong with you, little buddy?
   (D) Why are your nails so long?

4. Which statement is false?
   (A) Billy was an ordinary butterfly.
   B. Billy was an intelligent butterfly.
   C. Billy was a butterfly that could talk.
   D. Billy knew his way around in the forest.

5. Why was Nails afraid to cross the tree log that had fallen across the stream?
   A. Nails was afraid of heights and trees.
   (B) Cats do not like to get wet.
   C. Nails was just a beginner swimmer, and he was afraid he might fall into the water.
   D. Nails did not trust Billy; he thought Billy would push him into the water.

6. What color was Billy?
   A. black and white　　　B. yellow and brown
   (C) yellow and black　　　D. black and purple

7. What conclusion can you draw after reading the story of Nails?
   A. From now on, Nails will never chase another butterfly as long as he lives.
   B. From now on, Nails will never travel anywhere without his parents.
   C. From now on, Nails will be swimming in the stream every day.
   (D) From now on, Nails probably will have more confidence in himself.

8. "He (Billy) was quite intelligent, as intelligent as Albert Einstein," is an example of:
   (A) a simile　　　　　　　B. a pun
   C. a metaphor　　　　　　D. a personification

© Carson-Dellosa CD-2205　| Total Problems: ___ Total Correct: ___ Score: ___ |　**39**

Name _____ How Time Flies

Read the passage and answer the questions that follow. Circle the letter beside the correct answer.

How Time Flies

Close your eyes. Count to ten. Now open your eyes. That is almost how quickly life can pass you by. Just yesterday, it seems, the most important thing in the world to me was mastering the art of riding a bicycle. If I could just learn how, I thought, then everything would be right in the world. When I finally learned, happiness was all around me, covering me like a protective bubble. How quickly things change. Now, I hardly remember the last time I even sat on a bicycle.

The things that had once been so important, now seem trifles, and there is hardly time even to think of them, much less enjoy them. There is no time for the long ago, warm summer days on the back porch with watermelon juice from head to toe, and no time to roll and tumble in a field of newly cut hay. There is no time to take a short hike in the woods, to plant a little flower bed in the spring, to help my dad mow and rake the lawn on a summer day, or to climb a tree and swing down again.

Oh, how I took those days for granted. If only I had known they would go by so quickly. Rarely is there time to reflect and remember. It seems life always has me by the collar, pulling me in one direction or the other. I was so carefree in elementary and middle school, but now in high school with clubs, extracurricular activities, homework, chores at home, friends, and my part-time job, I seem to be too busy.

Maybe today I will go outside and ride my bike. I think I still know how to do it. Today is going to be my day. I am going to ride my bike, smell the air, climb a tree, and just sit there and think.

1. In the first paragraph, "happiness was all around me, covering me like a protective bubble." The word "happiness" is compared to:
   A. me　　　　　　　　　B. a covering
   (C) a bubble　　　　　　　D. a bicycle

2. Approximately how old is the writer in the above passage?
   A. 20-25 years old　　　(B) 15-18 years old
   C. 7-12 years old　　　　D. 30-35 years old

3. The main idea in the passage above is:
   (A) Sometimes we may take life for granted.
   B. Growing up now is difficult for teenagers.
   C. Everyone should learn to ride a bicycle.
   D. The older you get, the more you enjoy sports.

40　| Total Problems: ___ Total Correct: ___ Score: ___ |　© Carson-Dellosa CD-2205

Page 41 — Brown Coat Angel

Name _____   Brown Coat Angel

Read the passage and answer the questions that follow. Circle the letter beside the correct answer.

Brown Coat Angel

A boy and a few of his friends were in the woods playing a game of "capture the flag." They were having a great time. Suddenly, there was a clap of thunder like the sound of his grandfather's hammer. Rain began to fall between the cracks in the canopy of the forest. All of the boys began to hurry home in hopes that they would not get too wet. However, one boy tripped over a log and fell into a steep-sided creek. None of the others even noticed.

The rain began to fall harder and harder. The boy who was left behind was totally drenched. During his fall, he had sprained his ankle and could not climb out. He could feel the pain pulsing through his foot, but he tried to ignore it. He reached for a big stick that was lying near him and used it to help raise himself.

Just as the boy grabbed the stick, he heard some leaves rustling nearby. He turned his head and saw a man standing there. Wearing a long brown coat, the bearded man was tall and possibly in his late thirties. The stranger reached down and helped the young boy out of the creek. Once they reached the boy's house, the rain had stopped. The boy was glad to see his parents and turned around to thank the man. As he looked back, the boy saw nothing but the horizon in the distance.

1. A conclusion you could draw from the passage is:
   A. One should not play alone in the woods.
   B. The boy was helped by an angel.
   C. Playing "capture the flag" can be fun.
   D. One should avoid the outdoors during a lightning storm.

2. "There was a clap of thunder like the sound of his grandfather's hammer." The clap of thunder is compared to the sound of his grandfather's hammer. This writing technique is called:
   A. pun
   B. metaphor
   C. simile
   D. personification

Total Problems:____ Total Correct:____ Score:____ **41**

© Carson-Dellosa CD-2205

Page 42 — Waiting Her Whole Life

Name _____   Waiting Her Whole Life

Read the passage and answer the questions on the following page.

Waiting Her Whole Life

It seemed that Claire had been waiting her whole life for this day. However, in reality, it had been only five months since she had met John. It was possible that it seemed longer because from the moment she met him, her life had changed. From the first moment of their meeting, she had been waiting for this date to come. There was one thing for sure. She certainly had not realized that it would take so much work. Those who had done this before had told her it would be difficult at times, but Claire had smiled in self-assurance. She just knew it would be different for John and her. But her self-assurance turned out to be only the inexperience of her youth.

As the final days drew near, there was so much to do to make everything perfect. Claire spent many sleepless nights tossing and turning, too worried to sleep. Some nights she did not even make it to her bed. She was up all night preparing for the big day. The sleepless nights would sometimes result in Claire becoming very emotional around John, and this concerned him. Claire was certain that he was making the process more difficult than it should be, but John had his own peculiar ways and ideas.

When the day finally came, it was a beautiful spring morning. The air was so fresh and bright. Claire was nervous, but at the same time in a state of perfect bliss. It was to begin at 11:00 A.M. She walked slowly through the crowd of students, knowing that at the end of her walk, John would be there, waiting on her. Still, she was a little worried. There were so many details to remember. Had she done everything she needed to do to be prepared?

In retrospect, Claire could not see how she had ever made it through that hour and a half, but somehow she did. It lasted longer than she had wanted—ending at 12:15. Relieved and anxious, she was finally able to walk out to the sound of the ringing bell. Turning to her friend, she said, "Thank goodness, I'm through with chemistry for the semester. I hope I didn't fail that final. Come on, Amanda. Let's get some lunch. I'm starved."

42 © Carson-Dellosa CD-2205

Page 43 — Waiting Her Whole Life

Name _____   Waiting Her Whole Life

Read each question. Circle the letter beside the correct question.

1. The story is about Claire and:
   A. John on their wedding day
   B. John on their first date
   C. her chemistry semester test
   D. Amanda on their first day in high school

2. Another word or expression for "retrospect," in the last paragraph, is:
   A. inspection   B. the past
   C. looking back   D. the present

3. One can draw the conclusion that John is the:
   A. future husband   B. best friend's brother
   C. date   **D. teacher**

4. In the first paragraph, the expression "Those who had done this before had told her it would be difficult at times" means:
   A. Those who had planned a wedding before had found the preparations sometimes difficult and stressful.
   B. Those who had gone out on their first date would find the experience difficult and stressful.
   C. Those who had taken chemistry before had found the course to be difficult.
   D. Those who had met Amanda had found her to be difficult at times.

5. One can conclude that Claire is in high school because:
   A. She is taking a chemistry class.   B. She has her first date.
   C. She is nervous.   D. She has much homework.

6. Which one of the following happened first?
   A. Let's get some lunch.
   B. Claire spent many sleepless nights tossing and turning.
   C. She walked slowly through the crowd of people.
   D. She was finally able to walk out to the sound of the ringing bell.

Total Problems:____ Total Correct:____ Score:____ **43**

© Carson-Dellosa CD-2205

Page 44 — The Tree House

Name _____   The Tree House

Read the passage and answer the questions that follow. Circle the letter beside the correct answer.

The Tree House

Jan was sitting on the bottom step of her tree house ladder. Although it was a bitter autumn day, she was not wearing a coat because coats were for babies. Her best friend Belinda was wearing a new burgundy sweater that her aunt had bought her the day before. Because the air was cutting their lungs, they decided to go up into the old tree house. The tree house had been built eleven years ago when Jan turned one year old. Since then, she had painted it every summer and kept it fairly clean. The roof was black and the outer walls a very light sky blue. The ladder was brown and twisted like a screw. The one big room had brown carpet so that dirt would not show as much. Over the years, the girls had added furniture to the house. There was a small rocking chair that was handed down from Jan's grandmother, a coffee table, and a beanbag chair in the corner. When they spent the weekends together, the tree house was like a home to Jan and Belinda. The house was also a place where they could get away from everyone and sort out their problems.

1. The one big room in the tree house is described as having:
   A. a beanbag chair, rocking chair, black carpet, and a coffee table
   B. a rocking chair, beanbag chair, brown carpet, and an end table
   C. a beanbag chair, brown carpet, a rocking chair, and a coffee table
   D. a coffee table, brown carpet, beanbag chair, and a straight chair

2. "The ladder was brown and twisted like a screw." In this sentence, the ladder is compared to a:
   A. brown color
   B. screw
   C. twist
   D. not given

3. "The house had been built eleven years ago when Jan turned one year old." How old is Jan now?
   A. 11 years old
   B. 13 years old
   C. 10 years old
   D. 12 years old

44 Total Problems:____ Total Correct:____ Score:____

© Carson-Dellosa CD-2205

© Carson-Dellosa CD-2205

Name _____   Writing an Essay

Read the passage and answer the questions that follow. Circle the letter beside the correct answer.

Writing an Essay

Writing an essay or composition can be easy and fun if you follow a few procedures. First, write a relatively short introduction of three to four sentences. The purpose of the opening paragraph is to introduce the topic to the reader. The thesis statement or main idea of the whole paper is found in the introduction, and is usually the last sentence.

The next major part of the essay is called the supporting paragraphs. You should have at least two supporting paragraphs with at least five sentences in each paragraph. Each supporting paragraph begins with a topic sentence, which introduces the main idea for that paragraph. Supporting paragraphs contain details, facts, examples, passages, and quotes that support or reinforce your thesis statement.

The last major part of the essay is called the concluding paragraph. This last paragraph is also short—maybe three or four sentences. The purpose of the concluding paragraph is to bring the essay to a close. The first sentence is the restated thesis statement in which you write your thesis statement again, but in different words. The idea here is to bring the whole paper back together, to refocus and conclude.

1. The last part of the essay is called the:
   A. supporting paragraphs
   Ⓑ concluding paragraph
   C. thesis statement
   D. introduction

2. Each supporting paragraph contains:
   A. three sentences
   B. a thesis statement
   Ⓒ a topic sentence
   D. a restated thesis statement

3. An essay contains how many major parts?
   Ⓐ 3   B. 2
   C. 4   D. 5

4. Supporting paragraphs contain all but one of the following:
   A. facts   B. examples
   C. details   Ⓓ a thesis statement

© Carson-Dellosa CD-2205 | Total Problems: | Total Correct: | Score: | **45**

Name _____   Canada: A Parliamentary Democracy

Read the passage and answer the questions on the following page.

Canada: A Parliamentary Democracy

Canada is a parliamentary democracy. The country has a national legislature called Parliament, which meets in Ottawa, the national capital. The Canadian Parliament is composed of the House of Commons and the Senate. Representatives of the lower house, the House of Commons, are elected. Members of the upper house, the Senate, are appointed by the governor general.

The leader of Canada's national government is the prime minister. A prime minister is the leader of the political party that has a majority of members in the House of Commons. A majority is more than half the total number.

In Canada, the prime minister heads both the executive and the legislative branches of government. The two branches are not separate in Canada as they are in the United States. The prime minister governs with the help of the cabinet. The cabinet is comprised of the prime minister and about 30 members of the House of Commons. The cabinet members advise the prime minister and help him or her carry out the law.

The principle political parties include the Liberal Party, the Progressive Conservative Party, and the New Democratic Party. The major regional parties include the British Columbia Social Credit Party and the Parti Quebecois—important mainly in Quebec. Some prime ministers include Pierre Trudeau, from 1968-1979 and 1980-1984, and Brian Mulroney, from 1984-1988.

The prime minister depends on the support of Parliament to stay in office. Without the support from Parliament, the prime minister must resign. A prime minister did resign after several events in 1988, when important members of the government were criticized for "betraying the people."

Canada is one of the members of the Commonwealth of Nations, a group of independent nations once ruled by Great Britain. Commonwealth nations think of the British monarch—the king or queen—as the head of their governments. A monarchy is any government headed by a hereditary ruler, such as a king or queen. However, in Canada the British monarch is the leader in name only.

In Canada, the British monarch is represented by an official called the governor general. The governor general has little power. For the most part, this official approves decisions made by Parliament and the prime minister.

46   © Carson-Dellosa CD-2205

Name _____   Canada: A Parliamentary Democracy

Answer the questions below. Circle the letter beside the correct answer if appropriate.

1. The main idea of the descriptive passage is that:
   A. Brian Mulroney was the best prime minister in Canada's history.
   B. Canada has a very strict monarchy headed by Pierre Trudeau.
   Ⓒ Canada has a parliamentary democracy.
   D. The prime minister advises the cabinet members in carrying out the law.

2. The Canadian Parliament is composed of which two branches of government?
   Ⓐ Senate and House of Commons
   B. Senate and Liberal Party
   C. Parti Quebecois and Congress
   D. House of Representatives and Senate

3. A "monarchy" is:
   A. any government headed by a prime minister
   B. any government headed by a president
   C. a majority of the members in the House of Commons
   Ⓓ any government headed by a hereditary ruler, such as a king or queen

4. What are the names of five political parties in Canada? <u>Liberal Party,</u>
   <u>Progressive Conservative Party, New Democratic Party,</u>
   <u>British Columbia Social Credit Party, Parti Quebecois</u>

5. What is another name for the lower house in the Canadian Parliament?
   A. Liberal Party   Ⓑ House of Commons
   C. Senate   D. New Democratic Party

6. A prime minister is the leader of:
   A. the political party that has a minority of members in the House of Commons
   Ⓑ the political party that has a majority of members in the House of Commons
   C. the political party that is appointed by the Queen of England
   D. the political party that has a minority of members in the Senate

7. Canada's Parliament meets in their capital city of <u>Ottawa</u> .

8. What are the two components of the Canadian cabinet? <u>the prime minister and</u>
   <u>about 30 members of the House of Commons</u>

© Carson-Dellosa CD-2205 | Total Problems: | Total Correct: | Score: | **47**

Name _____   Wilton N. "Wilt" Chamberlain

Read the passage and answer the questions on the following page.

Wilton N. "Wilt" Chamberlain

A large and powerful man at 7'1", Wilt Chamberlain was considered by many to be the greatest offensive player in basketball history. Wilt's arrival into the league revolutionized the center position. His 100-point game against the New York Knicks on March 2, 1962, is an incredible record which will probably never be broken.

Wilt "The Stilt" Chamberlain was born in Philadelphia, Pennsylvania, on August 21, 1936. Coming out of high school, Wilt was a highly regarded player and had his choice of universities. He decided to attend the University of Kansas, where he led the Jayhawks to the 1957 NCAA tournament finals.

After leaving the University of Kansas, he briefly toured with the Harlem Globetrotters before joining the Philadelphia Warriors in 1959. He made an immediate impact there, winning both the Rookie of the Year and the MVP awards in his first season. He averaged an amazing 38 points and 27 rebounds per game. He went on to win a championship with the Philadelphia 76ers in 1967.

In 1968, Chamberlain went to the Los Angeles Lakers, where he teamed up with Jerry West to bring a championship to Los Angeles. This was a very talented Lakers team, but their championship hopes were constantly thwarted by the Boston Celtics. However, in 1972 Wilt and the Lakers won the championship. During this season, the Lakers set an NBA record, winning 33 straight games. Much of Chamberlain's early dominance was due to his tremendous size. But, during the later battles with the Celtics, Chamberlain showed he also possessed athleticism, speed, and unmatched basketball skills.

After fourteen seasons in the NBA, Chamberlain retired as a member of the Lakers in 1973. During his career, he won seven scoring titles, two NBA titles, and was named MVP of the league on four separate occasions. He is one of only two players to ever score over 30,000 points. On October 11, 1999, Chamberlain died of an apparent heart attack in California.

48   © Carson-Dellosa CD-2205

Page 49

Name _____   Wilton N. "Wilt" Chamberlain

Read each question. Circle the letter beside the correct answer.

1. In which city was Wilt Chamberlain born?
   A. Los Angeles   B. Kansas City
   C. Philadelphia   D. New York

2. Which event occurred first?
   A. The Lakers set an NBA record, winning 33 straight games.
   B. Coming out of high school, Wilt was a highly regarded player.
   C. He won both the Rookie of the Year and the MVP award.
   D. He won seven scoring titles and two NBA titles.

3. In what year did Chamberlain retire from the Lakers?
   A. 1973   B. 1972
   C. 1999   D. 1959

4. With which of the following teams did Chamberlain not play?
   A. Jayhawks   B. Atlanta Hawks
   C. Lakers   D. Harlem Globetrotters

5. Against which team did Chamberlain score 100 points?
   A. Philadelphia Warriors
   B. Los Angeles Lakers
   C. Harlem Globetrotters
   D. New York Knicks

6. How tall was Wilt Chamberlain?
   A. 1'7"   B. 71"
   C. 7'1"   D. 117"

7. Before joining the Philadelphia Warriors, Wilt briefly toured with the:
   A. Philadelphia Warriors
   B. Los Angeles Lakers
   C. Harlem Globetrotters
   D. New York Knicks

8. What is another word for "thwarted" as used in the fourth paragraph: ". . . but their championship hopes were constantly thwarted by the Boston Celtics."
   A. confirmed   B. started
   C. opposed   D. encouraged

© Carson-Dellosa CD-2205   Total Problems: Total Correct: Score: **49**

Page 50

Name _____   Oceania: Islands of the Pacific

Read the passage and answer the questions on the following page.

Oceania: Islands of the Pacific

Oceania is a name used to refer to the widely scattered islands of the central and south Pacific; Australia and New Zealand are frequently included. Virtually all the islands are volcanic peaks built upon submerged volcanic bases.

Australia is the world's smallest continent, and it is also the oldest. It is about the same size as the United States, not including Alaska. The small continent of Australia is like an enormous island, with 23,000 miles of coastline. There are no volcanoes or rugged new mountains on the continent.

Another island found in Oceania is New Zealand which has everything from mountains and waterfalls to seashores and hot springs. New Zealand has two main islands, North Island and South Island. South Island is larger than North Island and has a major mountain range, the Southern Alps.

The islands of Oceania can be sorted into three main groups. The name of each group tells something about its islands.

Polynesia means "many islands," but the name makes most people think of a warm, sunny climate, palm trees, and sandy beaches. Polynesia includes Tahiti, American Samoa, and, far to the east, Easter Island. Hawaii, the western-most state of the United States, is located within the area of Polynesia. Polynesia is spread over a huge stretch of ocean, which covers about 15 million square miles. The isolation of the islands in this area, as well as their small size, have limited their economic development.

You can probably guess the size of the islands of Micronesia from the name. Micronesia means "tiny islands." Micronesia contains more than 2,000 islands. Most of these islands are atolls (a coral island or string of coral islands and reefs forming a ring that nearly encloses a lagoon).

Melanesia means "black islands," a name given to the islands possibly because of the dark vegetation of their hillsides. Melanesia lies south of the equator, west of Polynesia, and northeast of Australia. Fiji and the Solomon Islands are part of Melanesia. Papua New Guinea, the eastern half of the island of New Guinea, is the largest country in Melanesia. It has a rugged, mountainous terrain. Heavy rainfall in the mountains collects in streams that cross swamps and forests.

50   © Carson-Dellosa CD-2205

Page 51

Name _____   Oceania: Islands of the Pacific

Answer the following questions. Write your answers in the spaces provided.

1. Oceania can be sorted into three main groups: **Polynesia, Micronesia, Melanesia**

2. In addition to the three main groups, **Australia** and **New Zealand** are frequently included in Oceania.

3. Micronesia, which means, "**tiny islands**," contains more than 2,000 islands, most of which are atolls.

4. **Melanesia**, which lies south of the Equator, is a name given to the islands possibly because of the dark vegetation of their hillsides.

5. **Australia**, the world's smallest continent, is about the size of the United States, not including Alaska.

6. Another island found in Oceania is **New Zealand**, which has everything from mountains and waterfalls to seashores and hot springs.

7. Covering about 15 million square miles, **Polynesia** includes Tahiti, American Samoa, and Easter Island.

8. **Atolls** are coral islands and reefs forming a ring that nearly encloses a lagoon.

9. Name three of the islands that make up Melanesia: **Fiji, the Solomon Islands, New Guinea**

© Carson-Dellosa CD-2205   Total Problems: Total Correct: Score: **51**

Page 52

Name _____   Marilyn Monroe

Read the passage and answer the questions on the following page.

Marilyn Monroe

Marilyn Monroe, a popular female entertainer during the 1950s, was born on June 1, 1926 in Los Angeles. Her father, Edward Mortensen, and her mother, Gladys Baker, were unable to care for the little girl known as Norma Jean Baker. She spent most of her childhood in foster homes and orphanages.

Later in her life, she found work as a model. With her ambition to become an actress, Marilyn studied at the Actors Studio in New York City. During her acting career, she starred in such hits as *Niagara*, *Gentlemen Prefer Blondes*, and *How to Marry a Millionaire*. Even though she was busy as a model and actress, she still found time to marry three husbands.

Her first marriage of four years was to a seaman named James Daugherty. Her second marriage of nine months was to the major-league baseball player Joe DiMaggio. Her third marriage of almost five years was to the American playwright Arthur Miller.

Marilyn Monroe died in Los Angeles on August 5, 1962 from an overdose of sleeping pills. Her death was shocking and traumatic for the whole world. Even though Miss Monroe has been dead for over thirty-eight years, she is still considered an American icon by some people.

On October 27-28, 1999, the famous auction house Christie's of New York held one of its most famous auctions. The title of the auction was "The Personal Property of Marilyn Monroe." Sales for both days totaled over $13 million dollars. The highlight of the sale was the "Happy Birthday" dress that Marilyn wore at Madison Square Garden on May 19, 1962, to sing to President John F. Kennedy. The long white dress sold for $1,276,000 to "Gotta Have It," a collectibles gallery in New York.

Some other highlights of the famous Christie's auction included Marilyn's diamond and platinum eternity band that Joe DiMaggio gave her after their wedding in 1954. The ring was sold to an anonymous bidder for $772,500. Her baby grand piano sold for $662,000 and a Mexican cardigan sold for $167,500. Tommy Hilfiger, a famous contemporary designer, purchased three pairs of denim blue jeans for $42,550, worn by Marilyn in 1954 in the movie *River of No Return*.

Tony Curtis, a movie star who co-starred with Marilyn in *Some Like It Hot*, said in attending the auction that Marilyn would be "moved and stunned" that people "still love her."

52   © Carson-Dellosa CD-2205

Name _____   Marilyn Monroe

Read each question. Circle the letter beside the correct answer.

1. At the Christie's auction, Marilyn Monroe's famous "Happy Birthday" dress sold for:
   A. $772,500
   B. $662,000
   C. $13,000,000
   (D) $1,276,000

2. Sales for both days at Christie's auction for the personal property of Marilyn totaled over:
   (A) $13,000,000
   B. $1,276,000
   C. $772,500
   D. $662,000

3. To whom did Marilyn sing "Happy Birthday" at Madison Square Garden?
   (A) President John F. Kennedy
   B. Joe DiMaggio
   C. Arthur Miller
   D. Tommy Hilfiger

4. Who gave Marilyn the ring that sold for $772,000.00?
   A. Tommy Hilfiger
   (B) Joe DiMaggio
   C. Arthur Miller
   D. President John F. Kennedy

5. Which one of the following is not a hit movie in which Marilyn starred?
   (A) *Sands of the Desert*
   B. *How to Marry a Millionaire*
   C. *Gentlemen Prefer Blondes*
   D. *Niagara*

6. Marilyn Monroe spent most of her young life in:
   A. Hollywood
   (B) orphanages and foster homes
   C. New York City
   D. Mexico

7. Another word that means the same as "icon," in the fourth paragraph, is:
   A. beauty
   B. actress
   (C) idol
   D. friend

8. Who bought Marilyn's blue jeans at the Christie's auction?
   A. President John F. Kennedy
   B. Joe DiMaggio
   C. Tony Curtis
   (D) Tommy Hilfiger

9. What was the reason for Monroe's death in 1962?
   A. car accident
   B. accidental drowning
   (C) overdose of sleeping pills
   D. filming accident

© Carson-Dellosa CD-2205 | Total Problems: | Total Correct: | Score: | **53**

Name _____   Puerto Rico: A State?

Read the passage and answer the questions on the following page.

Puerto Rico: A State?

Puerto Rico has been a self-governing commonwealth since 1952. As a commonwealth, Puerto Rico is a possession of the United States, but it is governed by its own constitution. Citizens of Puerto Rico have many of the rights and responsibilities of United States citizens; however, Puerto Ricans do not have the right to vote in national elections, and they are not required to pay federal taxes.

Some people in Puerto Rico are not satisfied with its status as a commonwealth. They want Puerto Rico to become a state of the United States. The movement to make Puerto Rico a state has gained wide support during recent years. Supporters believe that political, social, and economic conditions in Puerto Rico would improve if statehood were acquired. With statehood, Puerto Rico would be directly represented in the United States Senate and the House of Representatives. Federal funds would become available to provide housing and jobs for people who are unemployed there.

Baltasar Corrada del Rio, a former mayor of San Juan, explained that statehood would provide Puerto Rico with local self-government, as well as more political participation in Washington, D.C. As a state, Puerto Rico would continue to elect its own governor, as well as senators and representatives to its legislature. In addition, Puerto Ricans would be afforded equal participation in the United States Senate, fair representation in the House of Representatives, and a share in the responsibility to pay federal taxes. The island would also continue to have its two flags and its two anthems.

However, other Puerto Ricans believe that the island should remain a commonwealth. They feel that becoming part of the United States might cause them to lose their language and their culture. They believe that commonwealth status lets them keep and protect their Hispanic culture. They feel that if Puerto Rico becomes a state, Congress might impose English as their official language, an action which would lead to a lessening of the island's Hispanic culture. Among those who oppose the idea of Puerto Rican statehood are citizens who prefer to maintain the status quo and those who favor independence. The three main political parties in Puerto Rico reflect the preferences for statehood, status quo, and independence.

Miquel A. Herandez Agosto, former president of the Puerto Rican Senate, explained that Puerto Ricans are a Spanish-speaking people who cherish their Hispanic culture and would not exchange it for any material benefits. They are also proud of their linkage with the United States, but are not willing to relinquish Spanish as their first language nor to change their Hispanic culture for the "American way of life."

 54   © Carson-Dellosa CD-2205

Name _____   Puerto Rico: A State?

Read each question. Circle the letter beside the correct answer.

1. What is the main issue of this passage?
   (A) whether Puerto Rico should become a state or remain a possession of the United States
   B. whether Puerto Rico should pay federal taxes
   C. whether Puerto Rico should continue to have two flags and two anthems
   D. whether Puerto Rico should change its official language

2. What is the view of those Puerto Ricans in favor of statehood?
   A. Statehood would mean Puerto Rico would lose its language.
   B. Statehood would mean Puerto Rico would lose its culture.
   C. Statehood would mean losing their status quo.
   (D) Statehood would improve the political, social, and economic conditions in Puerto Rico.

3. What is the position of those Puerto Ricans who oppose statehood?
   A. Puerto Ricans would be afforded equal participation in the United States Senate.
   (B) Becoming part of the United States could cause Puerto Rico to lose its language and culture.
   C. Puerto Ricans would be available for federal housing and jobs.
   D. Puerto Rico would continue to have its two flags and its two anthems.

4. Puerto Rico has been a self-governing commonwealth since:
   A. 1950
   (B) 1952
   C. 1956
   D. 1958

5. If Puerto Rico were to become a state, it would continue to elect its own:
   (A) governor
   B. prime minister
   C. president
   D. king

6. If Puerto Rico were to become a state, some Puerto Ricans believe that English might be imposed as their official language by the United States:
   A. the Senate
   (B) Congress
   C. the House of Representatives
   D. Parliament

7. In the fourth paragraph, "status quo" means:
   A. a state
   B. unpopular
   C. a number
   (D) existing state of affairs

© Carson-Dellosa CD-2205 | Total Problems: | Total Correct: | Score: | **55**

Name _____   Hurricanes: Natural Disasters

Read the passage and answer the questions on the following page.

Hurricanes: Natural Disasters

A hurricane is a powerful, swirling storm that begins over a warm sea. When a hurricane hits land, it can cause great damage through fierce winds, torrential rain, flooding, and huge waves crashing ashore. A powerful hurricane can destroy more property than any other natural disaster.

The winds of a hurricane swirl around a calm central zone called the eye, which is surrounded by a band of tall, dark clouds called the eye wall. The eye is usually about 10 to 20 miles in diameter and is free of rain and large clouds. In the eye wall, large changes in pressure create the hurricane's strongest winds. These winds can reach 200 miles per hour. Damaging winds may extend 250 miles from the eye.

Hurricanes are referred to by different labels, depending on where they occur. They are called *hurricanes* when they happen over the North Atlantic Ocean, the Caribbean Sea, the Gulf of Mexico, or the Northeast Pacific Ocean. Such storms are known as *typhoons* if they occur in the Northwest Pacific Ocean. Near Australia and in the Indian Ocean, they are referred to as *tropical cyclones*.

Hurricanes are most common during the summer and early fall. In the Atlantic and the Northeast Pacific oceans, for example, August and September are the peak hurricane months. Typhoons occur throughout the year in the Northwest Pacific but are most frequent in summer. In the North Indian Ocean, tropical cyclones strike in May and November. In the South Indian Ocean, the South Pacific Ocean, and off the coast of Australia, the hurricane seasons run from December to March. Approximately 85 hurricanes, typhoons, and tropical cyclones occur each year throughout the world.

 56   © Carson-Dellosa CD-2205

© Carson-Dellosa CD-2205

Hurricanes: Natural Disasters

Name _____

Read each question. Circle the letter beside the correct answer.

1. What word refers to the calm, central zone which is surrounded by a band of tall, dark clouds?
   - A. eye
   - B. eye wall
   - C. hurricane
   - D. cyclone

2. Which one of the following statements is false?
   - A. Hurricanes occur over the North Atlantic Ocean.
   - B. Typhoons are frequent in the summer.
   - C. Hurricanes are common during the early fall.
   - D. Hurricanes occur over the Northwest Pacific Ocean.

3. What are the peak hurricane months in the Atlantic and Northeast Pacific areas?
   - A. August, October
   - B. September, November
   - C. August, September
   - D. June, July

4. Winds in hurricanes can reach speeds up to:
   - A. 250 miles per hour
   - B. 200 miles per hour
   - C. 20 miles per hour
   - D. 85 miles per hour

5. A hurricane begins:
   - A. when it hits land
   - B. with a cool front
   - C. over a warm sea
   - D. with thunder and lightning

6. A hurricane is called a hurricane when it happens over all but one of the following areas:
   - A. Caribbean Sea
   - B. Northwest Pacific Ocean
   - C. Gulf of Mexico
   - D. Northeast Pacific ocean

7. Damage from a hurricane may extend how far from the eye?
   - A. 85 miles
   - B. 250 miles
   - C. 20 miles
   - D. 200 miles

8. Approximately how many hurricanes, typhoons, and tropical cyclones occur each year?
   - A. 200
   - B. 85
   - C. 250
   - D. 20

| Total Problems: | Total Correct: | Score: | 57 |

Spain: Dictatorship to Democracy

Name _____

Read the passage and answer the questions that follow. Circle the letter beside each correct answer.

Spain: Dictatorship to Democracy

In 1975 Spain emerged from a long dictatorship to become a peaceful, democratic country. That year, Prince Juan Carlos became king of Spain. He took over after the death of Francisco Franco, who had ruled the country as a dictator.

Spain's government is somewhat different from the governments of other southern European countries. Although Spain is governed by an elected parliament, it also has a monarch. In this respect, Spain's government is like that of Great Britain.

Under Franco's rule, free elections and political parties had not been allowed in the country. When Juan Carlos came to power, the government of Spain was completely changed. First, the Spanish people elected a new parliament. Then, a new constitution was both written and approved in 1978. It established a parliamentary democracy with King Juan Carlos as head of the government.

Under the new constitution, the legislative branch—called the *Cortes*—is divided into two houses. Most of the power is in the lower house, called the Congress of Deputies, which is made up of 350 members elected by the people. The upper house is called the Senate.

1. Spain's government is similar to Great Britain's because both governments have a:
   - A. dictatorship
   - B. Senate
   - C. president
   - D. monarch

2. In what year did dictatorship end in Spain?
   - A. 1979
   - B. 1972
   - C. 1975
   - D. 350 A.D.

3. The first thing the Spanish people did after Carlos came to power was:
   - A. elect a new parliament
   - B. build a new palace
   - C. execute Franco
   - D. repeal the income tax

4. What two things were not allowed in the country under Franco's rule?
   - A. free elections, private businesses
   - B. free elections, political parties
   - C. political parties, private businesses
   - D. political parties, visiting dignitaries

5. What was the name of the Spanish dictator?
   - A. Juan Carlos
   - B. King Cortes
   - C. Francisco Franco
   - D. Great Britain

| 58 | Total Problems: | Total Correct: | Score: |

Making Chicken Gumbo Soup

Name _____

Refer to the recipe to answer the questions at the bottom of the page. Circle the letter beside each correct answer.

Making Chicken Gumbo Soup

Ingredients
- 1 stewing chicken
- 1 cup flour
- ¼ cup bacon drippings
- 4 cups boiling water
- 2 cups skinned, seeded tomatoes
- ½ cup fresh corn, cut from the cob
- 1 cup sliced okra
- 1 large green pepper—seeds and membrane removed, or 2 small red peppers
- ½ teaspoon salt
- ¼ cup diced onion
- ¼ cup uncooked rice
- 5 cups water

Directions
Cut the chicken into pieces and sprinkle with flour. Brown the meat in the bacon drippings. Pour the boiling water over the browned meat. Simmer, uncovered, until the meat falls from the bones. Strain the stock and reserve. Debone and chop the meat. Place the chopped meat and the stock in a soup kettle with the vegetables, rice, and additional water. Simmer, uncovered, about 30 minutes or until the vegetables are tender. Season to taste. Makes about 12 cups.

1. What is an appropriate substitution for the large green pepper?
   - A. 1 cucumber
   - B. 2 small red peppers
   - C. 2 squash
   - D. 3 chili peppers

2. How long do you simmer the meat after it has been chopped and placed in the soup kettle?
   - A. 5 minutes
   - B. 12 minutes
   - C. 30 minutes
   - D. 35 minutes

3. What is the first thing to do in making the soup?
   - A. Cut the chicken into pieces and sprinkle with flour.
   - B. Sprinkle the chicken gumbo with flour.
   - C. Add ¼ cup bacon drippings to 4 cups of hot water.
   - D. Boil 4 cups of water and add flour.

4. After the ingredients have cooked, approximately how many cups of soup will this make?
   - A. 2 cups
   - B. 5 cups
   - C. 4 cups
   - D. 12 cups

| Total Problems: | Total Correct: | Score: | 59 |

Growing Bread Mold

Name _____

Read the experiment. Circle the letter beside the correct answer.

Growing Bread Mold

Problem:	**Materials:**
Do hidden variables affect the results of an experiment?	slice of bread 2 jars with lids medicine dropper

Procedure:
1. Tear a slice of bread in half.
2. Place each half into a separate jar.
3. Use the medicine dropper to moisten each half with 10 drops of water. Cover the jars.
4. Place one jar in sunlight and the other jar in a dark closet.
5. Observe the jars every few days for about two weeks. Record your observations in a data table. Once the experiment is completed, what conclusion can you draw?

Observations:
1. Did you observe mold growth in either jar?
2. If so, describe any differences or similarities in mold growth in the two jars.
3. Do you think that light affects the growth of bread mold? If so, how?

1. Which necessary ingredient is not listed in the materials list?
   - A. mold
   - B. water
   - C. test tube
   - D. foil

2. According to the directions, one jar should be placed in a dark closet and the other jar placed in:
   - A. the kitchen
   - B. the science lab
   - C. a drawer of a desk
   - D. the sunlight

3. If you follow the directions, the first thing to do is:
   - A. Gather all the materials together on the kitchen counter or in the science lab.
   - B. Place 10 drops of water on each piece of bread.
   - C. Tear a slice of bread in half.
   - D. Fill each jar with 2 cups of water.

| 60 | Total Problems: | Total Correct: | Score: |

Name _____   Let's Make Caramel Cream Fudge

Refer to the recipe to answer the questions at the bottom of the page. Circle the letter beside each correct answer.

Let's Make Caramel Cream Fudge

Ingredients

1 cup brown sugar	2 tablespoons butter
1 cup sugar	1 teaspoon vanilla
1/8 teaspoon salt	1 cup broken black walnuts
1/3 cup corn syrup	2 teaspoons oil
1 cup milk	

Directions

(1) Place sugars, salt, corn syrup, and milk in a large, heavy pan. (2) Cook these ingredients quickly, stirring constantly until they boil. (3) Cook and stir 3 minutes. (4) Reduce the heat and cook until the mixture reaches the softball stage—230°. (5) Place the butter in the bottom of a mixing bowl. (6) Remove pan from heat and at once pour mixture over butter. Do not stir. (7) When cool, add vanilla and beat until creamy. (8) Just as the mixture loses its gloss, stir in the walnuts. Pour onto an oiled cutting board. (9) Cut into squares when set and store tightly covered.

1. After the ingredients have reached the boiling point, how many minutes should you cook and stir them?
   A. 2 minutes
   B. 3 minutes
   C. 4 minutes
   D. 5 minutes

2. What is the first thing you do in the directions?
   A. Cook all of the ingredients quickly, stirring them constantly.
   B. Place butter in the bottom of a mixing bowl or use an electric mixer.
   C. Put the ingredients in a large, heavy pan.
   D. Remove pan from heat and at once pour mixture over butter.

3. What ingredient is added in step 7?
   A. 1 teaspoon vanilla
   B. 1 cup broken black walnuts
   C. 2 tablespoons butter
   D. 1 cup brown sugar

4. After you have poured the mixture onto an oiled cutting board, what should you do next?
   A. Just as the mixture loses it gloss, stir in 1 cup broken black walnuts.
   B. Cut into squares when set and store tightly covered.
   C. When cool, add 1 teaspoon vanilla.
   D. Remove the lid, reduce the heat, and cook until mixture reaches a softball stage.

© Carson-Dellosa CD-2205 | Total Problems: ___ Total Correct: ___ Score: ___ | **61**

Name _____   Matter In Ocean Water

Read the experiment. Circle the letter beside the correct answer.

Matter In Ocean Water

Problem:
Do you know from where some kinds of matter in ocean water come?

Materials:
You will need some clean sand, a jar with a screw top, two milk cartons, a large needle, and some table salt. You will also need a teaspoon, two paper cups, four blocks of wood, a measuring cup, and some water.

Procedure:
1. Wash the sand by putting it into the jar with clean water. Then, screw the top on so that it fits well and shake the jar several times.
2. Let the jar stand for a few minutes, and carefully pour off only the water. Wash the sand in this way two more times so that the sand will be very clean.
3. Cut the top off each milk carton. With the large needle, make five or six holes in the bottom of each carton.
4. Add washed sand to each carton until it is about two-thirds full. Then, mix a teaspoon of table salt with the sand in one of the cartons. Now, place both cartons on wooden blocks over the cups.
5. Pour 50 ml of water into each carton. Let the water flow through the sand into each cup.

Observations:
1. Will the water in both cups look the same?
2. Where do you think some of the matter in ocean water comes from?

1. After placing the sand into a jar with clean water, you then:
   A. Let the jar stand for a few minutes.
   B. Wash the sand several times and let stand.
   C. Clean the sand, using the two milk cartons and table salt.
   D. Screw the top and shake the jar.

2. All of the following materials are needed except:
   A. two milk cartons and two paper cups   **B. a ruler and a tablespoon**
   C. a measuring cup and water   D. sand and a large needle

3. The last procedure is:
   A. to let the jar stand for a few minutes and pour off only the water
   B. to pour 50 ml of water into each carton
   C. to mix a teaspoon of table salt with the sand in one of the cartons
   D. to make five or six holes in the bottom of each carton

62 | Total Problems: ___ Total Correct: ___ Score: ___ | © Carson-Dellosa CD-2205

Name _____   Making Banana Pudding

Read the recipe and answer the questions that follow. Circle the letter beside the correct answer.

Making Banana Pudding

Ingredients
1 cup sugar (separated into 3/4 and 1/4 cup)
1/3 cup all-purpose flour
1/4 teaspoon salt
2 cups milk, scalded
2 eggs, separated
1 teaspoon vanilla extract
25 vanilla wafers
4 bananas, sliced

Directions
(1) Combine 3/4 sugar, flour, and salt in top of double boiler. Mix well and stir in milk. (2) Cook about 15 minutes, stirring constantly. (3) Beat the egg yolks until thick and lemon-colored. (4) Gradually stir one-fourth of the hot mixture into the yolks; add remaining hot mixture, stirring constantly. (5) Cook 2 minutes longer. Remove from heat and add vanilla. Cool. (6) Line a 1-quart baking dish with half of the vanilla wafers. Next, add a layer of sliced bananas. (7) Top with half of the pudding. Repeat layers. (8) Beat egg whites until soft peaks form. Then gradually add 1/4 cup sugar and beat until stiff. Spread meringue over the pudding and bake at 350° for 15 minutes. Servings: 6

1. All the following are false for step 5, except one:
   A. Cook 1 minute longer.
   B. Remove from heat and add wafers.
   C. Cool.
   D. Line a 1-quart baking dish with half of the bananas.

2. In which step do you add a layer of bananas?
   A. step 7   B. step 8
   C. step 5   **D. step 6**

3. Which of the following statements is true for step 1?
   A. Combine flour, salt, and eggs in top of double boiler.
   B. Combine salt, flour, and sugar in top of double boiler.
   C. Combine 1/2 cup sugar, flour, and milk in top of double boiler.
   D. Combine flour, salt, and vanilla in top of double boiler.

© Carson-Dellosa CD-2205 | Total Problems: ___ Total Correct: ___ Score: ___ | **63**

Name _____   A Carpet's Point of View

Read the poem and answer the questions that follow. Circle the letter beside the correct answer.

A Carpet's Point of View

Mine is a humble existence;
I'm here to cover the floor.
Occasionally, I get vacuumed,
and I ask for nothing more.

Parties are what I really hate,
getting trampled and worn.
So many spills and so much wear,
I look shabby and forlorn.

Time has passed and now I'm old.
Soon, I will be replaced,
but I've collected memories,
and those cannot be erased.

Winter was my favorite season,
when children would lie down, warm and snug.
They'd brush my fur with their tiny hands,
and I felt like more than a rug.

Mine is a humble existence though;
I'm just here to cover the floor.
I've served my purpose with comfort and love,
and could ask for nothing more.

1. Winter was the carpet's favorite season because:
   A. Children would lie on it and make it feel like a rug.
   B. Children would lie on it and make it feel like more than a rug.
   C. Children would lie on it and spill drinks on it.
   D. They would vacuum it and make it feel worn.

2. The carpet appears to be human throughout the poem in all except one of the following examples:
   A. ... and I felt like more than a rug.
   B. I ask for nothing more.
   C. ... getting trampled and worn.
   D. Mine is a humble existence.

64 | Total Problems: ___ Total Correct: ___ Score: ___ | © Carson-Dellosa CD-2205

Name _____ The First Day of Spring

Read the poem and answer the questions that follow. Circle the letter beside the correct answer.

The First Day of Spring

I look out the window to see the grass;
the grass is no longer the color of brass.
There are birds in the trees
and there are honeybees.

The first day of spring is here,
so that means that summer is near.
It is the day of the happy farmer,
because he knows the days will be warmer.

The days are long
like the birds' songs.
It is the first day of spring,
and the birds are ready to sing.

1. "The days are long/like the birds' songs." In this line the days are compared to songs. What is the writing technique when one thing is compared to another thing using the word "like"?
   A. metaphor   B. symbol
   C. pun   (D) simile

2. Why is the farmer happy?
   A. because the grass is getting greener
   (B) because the weather is getting warmer
   C. because he does not like the winter
   D. because he has a new tractor

3. When two words sound the same, as "grass" and "brass" do, this is called:
   A. rhythm   B. simile
   (C) rhyme   D. poetry

4. "The First Day of Spring" contains:
   A. three lines   (B) three stanzas
   C. twelve verses   D. twelve stanzas

© Carson-Dellosa CD-2205 | Total Problems: | Total Correct: | Score: | **65**

Name _____ What Would We Do?

Read the poem and answer the questions on the following page.

What Would We Do?

What would we do
without the light of the sun?
Where would we go,
and how would we get there?

What would we do
without the flowers and trees?
What would we see,
and what would we smell?

What would we do
without the rivers and streams?
How would we live,
and what would we taste?

What would we do
without the birds and the bees?
What would we hear,
and what would we sing?

What would we do
without the moon and the stars?
What would we dream,
and how would we feel?

What would we do
without the animals on earth?
Who would instruct us
and how would we know?

What would we do
without the heavens and earth?
To feed us and guide us
along nature's wonder of ways.

66 | © Carson-Dellosa CD-2205

Name _____ What Would We Do?

Read each question. Circle the letter beside the correct answer.

1. According to the poet, specifically, what do the heavens and earth do for us?
   A. They help us to see and smell everything around us.
   (B) They feed us and guide us along nature's wonder of ways.
   C. They help us to hear, sing, and taste everything around us.
   D. They instruct us and make our dreams come true.

2. The poet believes that the moon and the stars provide humans with an opportunity to:
   A. teach and think
   B. hear and sing
   (C) dream and feel
   D. see and smell

3. In the last stanza, another word for "heavens" would be:
   A. God   (B) universe
   C. stars   D. planets

4. The poet believes that birds and bees provide humans with an opportunity to:
   (A) hear and sing   B. dream and feel
   C. see and smell   D. teach and know

5. Every stanza has two questions, except stanza:
   A. # 1   B. # 5
   C. # 3   (D) # 7

6. In stanza # 2, what senses are mentioned?
   A. sight and hearing   (B) sight and smell
   C. hearing and taste   D. hearing and touch

7. Which one of the following statements could possibly be the main idea?
   A. The light of the sun is something we couldn't live without.
   B. Flowers, trees, birds, and bees are things we couldn't live without.
   (C) Nature is all around us, yet we don't seem to realize we couldn't live without it.
   D. The animals teach us how to live each day of our lives.

8. A word that means the opposite of the word "wonder" in stanza # 7 is:
   (A) ordinary   B. star
   C. amazement   D. think

© Carson-Dellosa CD-2205 | Total Problems: | Total Correct: | Score: | **67**

Name _____ Morning

Read the poem and answer the questions that follow. Circle the letter beside the correct answer.

Morning

The soldiers of the dawn
ride on the sun's rays.
Slowly they take the day
like a helpless pawn.
They bathe themselves
in the dew that cleanses
the Earth anew.
Retreating, they take
the light captive,
only to return it
the next day.

1. "The soldiers of the dawn/ride on the sun's rays." The soldiers are under the command of:
   A. the moon   B. the general
   (C) the sun   D. the president

2. In line 1, the word "soldier" is a writing technique called:
   A. simile   B. alliteration
   C. setting   (D) metaphor

3. Regarding "they bathe themselves," in line five: who is they?
   A. dew   (B) soldiers
   C. animals   D. plants

4. What is the meaning of the word "retreating" in line eight?
   (A) withdrawing   B. forcing
   C. surrendering   D. hearing

5. Which word rhymes with "dawn"?
   A. take   B. rays
   (C) pawn   D. day

68 | Total Problems: | Total Correct: | Score: | © Carson-Dellosa CD-2205

93

Name _____ O Christmas Tree

Read the poem and answer the questions that follow. Circle the letter beside the correct answer.

O Christmas Tree

It was the night before Christmas,
and the tree was sparkling like a diamond in the sun,
with ornaments glittering and glistening in the light,
while tiny bulbs, like a million jewels, were dancing everywhere.

Crowned by an angel, the tree was protected and guarded.
Looking at the tree, I was filled with unbelievable sensations.
Suddenly to my horror and dismay the angel toppled,
ornaments shattered like glass and little bulbs cracked like lightning.

Waiting for the light show to end, I gazed in disbelief,
as my kitty sat watching and looking at me
with huge yellow eyes and a big happy grin.
She had a look on her face that was worth a million.

Picking her up out of the muddle and leaving everything behind,
quickly darting off to bed,
I left my parents to recover and recollect,
as my kitty and I wait for Santa.

1. Paying attention to the context clues surrounding the word, choose another word that means the same as "muddle" in line 13.
   A. mud puddle   (B) mess
   C. blood   D. water

2. What causes the Christmas tree to topple?
   A. a cat   (B) the angel
   C. too many lights   D. Santa Claus

3. The tiny bulbs on the tree are compared to:
   A. an angel   B. a cat
   (C) jewels   D. the sun

4. What is protecting and guarding the tree?
   A. lightning   (B) angel
   C. kitty   D. poet

© Carson-Dellosa CD-2205 | Total Problems: | Total Correct: | Score: | **69**

Name _____ A Seat on a Bus

Read the poem and answer the questions that follow. Circle the letter beside the correct answer.

A Seat on a Bus

As I sat there
on the bus that day,
I was very tired
with not a whole lot to say.
You told me to get up,
and I did not know what to do.
You are a white man;
I'm supposed to listen to you.
I am tired of all the things they say
about the problems
in our nation today.
I saw the look you gave
when I wouldn't meet your demand.
But for a person like me
you'd never lend a hand.
I'm not disrespectful; I mean,
I'm not trying to be.
I am trying to make a point
that I hope you can see.
I didn't mean any trouble,
a fight, or a fuss.
And all of this happened
over a seat on a bus.

1. According to the poem, what did the speaker do when asked to "get up"?
   A. stood up   (B) didn't get up
   C. started a fight   D. kept reading a newspaper

2. You can draw the conclusion that the speaker in the poem is:
   A. white   B. an old person
   (C) black   D. a student

3. The main idea of the poem is:
   A. A white person should be able to sit anywhere on a bus.
   B. Fights and fusses can often erupt on a bus.
   C. Blacks and whites cannot get along on a bus.
   (D) Any person, black or white, should be allowed to sit anywhere on a bus.

70 | Total Problems: | Total Correct: | Score: | © Carson-Dellosa CD-2205

Name _____ Reading a Pie Graph

Refer to the graph to answer each question. Write each answer in the space provided.

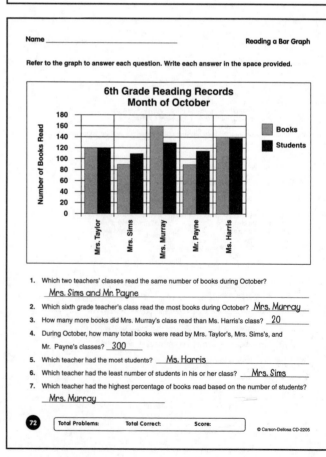

Types of Jobs in the United States

Transportation and Communication 7.0%
Finance and Real Estate 6.5%
Construction 6.5%
Government 4.7%
Services 31.0%
Manufacturing and Mining 20.4%
Trade 20.9%
Agriculture 3.0%

1. What does the whole circle graph represent? _types of jobs in the United States_

2. What are the three largest categories of jobs found in the United States?
   A. _services_ , B. _trade_ ,
   and C. _manufacturing and mining_ .

3. In which category are most workers employed? _services_

4. Which area employs the smallest number of workers? _agriculture_

5. Approximately _20.4_ % of the nation's workers have jobs in manufacturing and mining.

6. Finance and real estate employ _6.5_ % of the nation's workers.

© Carson-Dellosa CD-2205 | Total Problems: | Total Correct: | Score: | **71**

Name _____ Reading a Bar Graph

Refer to the graph to answer each question. Write each answer in the space provided.

**6th Grade Reading Records
Month of October**

Number of Books Read (0–180)

Legend: Books, Students

Mrs. Taylor, Mrs. Sims, Mrs. Murray, Mr. Payne, Ms. Harris

1. Which two teachers' classes read the same number of books during October?
   Mrs. Sims and Mr. Payne

2. Which sixth grade teacher's class read the most books during October? _Mrs. Murray_

3. How many more books did Mrs. Murray's class read than Ms. Harris's class? _20_

4. During October, how many total books were read by Mrs. Taylor's, Mrs. Sims's, and Mr. Payne's classes? _300_

5. Which teacher had the most students? _Ms. Harris_

6. Which teacher had the least number of students in his or her class? _Mrs. Sims_

7. Which teacher had the highest percentage of books read based on the number of students?
   Mrs. Murray

72 | Total Problems: | Total Correct: | Score: | © Carson-Dellosa CD-2205

Page 73 — Reading a Line Graph

Name _____ Reading a Line Graph

Refer to the graph to answer each question. Write each answer in the space provided.

Frankie's Dress Shop Monthly Electric Bills

(Cost in Dollars, 0–260; months Jan–Dec)

1. Which month had the highest cost in electricity? **August**
   Why? **answers will vary**

2. Which month had the lowest bill? **March** Why? **answers will vary**

3. Which 3 months had the same electric bills? **Jan., Apr., Dec.**

4. If Frankie's Dress Shop was in Appleton, Wisconsin, instead of Atlanta, Georgia, how might the graph differ during August? **The electric bill may be lower if the shop were in Wisconsin.**

5. How might Frankie's Dress Shop use this graph for future planning? **answers will vary**

6. Explain the fluctuations in the graph. **answers will vary**

Total Problems: Total Correct: Score: **73**
© Carson-Dellosa CD-2205

Page 74 — Library and Reference Skills

Name _____ Library and Reference Skills

Read each question. Circle the letter beside the correct answer.

1. If you had to find a word that has the same meaning as "somber," you would look in:
   A. an encyclopedia   B. a telephone directory   **(C) a thesaurus**   D. an atlas

2. Your family is going to the island of Crete, and you don't know where this island is located. To find out where this island is located in the world, you probably would look in:
   A. a biographical dictionary   B. a thesaurus   **(C) an atlas**   D. a card catalog

3. Suppose your science teacher suggests your class plant a watermelon field in the spring. If she wants you to plant the watermelon seeds at the right time of the moon, you would consult:
   A. Bartlett's Book of Quotations   **(B) The Farmer's Almanac**   C. National Geographic Atlas   D. Reader's Guide to Periodical Literature

4. In which section of the newspaper would you find "help wanted" ads?
   A. sports section   **(B) classified section**   C. entertainment section   D. front page

5. Your English teacher asked you to find the meaning of "turbulence." You would look in:
   A. an atlas   B. a thesaurus   **(C) a dictionary**   D. an encyclopedia

6. You are doing research on the Biltmore Estate near Asheville, North Carolina. If you wanted general information on this famous house, you could look in:
   (A) an encyclopedia   B. Reader's Guide to Periodical Literature   C. a thesaurus   D. an international Who's Who?

7. In a book, where do you find the title, author, and publisher?
   A. index   **(B) title page**   C. glossary   D. table of contents

8. If your teacher asked you to bring in recent information on the president and one of his recent trips abroad, you would probably look in:
   A. an encyclopedia   B. a card catalog   C. a dictionary   **(D) a newspaper**

74 Total Problems: Total Correct: Score: © Carson-Dellosa CD-2205

Page 75 — Reading the Dictionary

Name _____ Reading the Dictionary

Refer to the dictionary entry to answer each question. Circle the letter beside the correct answer.

home, (hom) n. 1. the place where a person lives; one's dwelling place. 2. the city, state, or country where one was born or reared. 3. a place where one likes to be; restful or congenial place. 4. one's final resting place; the grave. 5. the members of a family; household or the life around it. 6. an institution for orphans, the infirmed, aged, etc. 7. the natural environment, or habitat, of an animal, plant, etc. adj. 1. of one's home or country; domestic. 2. of, or at the center of operations: as, a home office. 3. to the point; effective. adv. 1. at, to, or in the direction of home. 2. to the point aimed at: as, he drove the nail home. 3. to the center or heart of a matter; closely.

1. What is the part of speech for the definition of "home" that means "at the center of operations"?
   A. adverb   B. verb   **(C) adjective**   D. noun

2. Which numbered definition means "the members of a family"?
   A. 6   **(B) 5**   C. 3   D. 2

3. What is definition # 7 for the word "home"?
   A. institution for orphans   B. of one's home or country   C. one's dwelling place   **(D) natural environment of an animal**

4. In which sentence below is the word "home" used as a noun?
   A. The corporate lawyer's home office is located in San Francisco.
   B. Jan ran home to see if she left her library books on the dining room table.
   (C) Ian's home is situated between two rolling hills of green grass and heather.
   D. The home box office was closed when we were there at 4:00 this afternoon.

5. In which sentence below is the word "home" used as an adjective?
   A. I need to go home to check with my grandmother before I go to the movie.
   (B) At halftime, the home team's score was tied with the opposing team's score.
   C. My dad left his new boots at home and couldn't climb the steep mountain.
   D. Grandma boarded the plane and said to the pilot, "Steer this plane home. I'm tired."

Total Problems: Total Correct: Score: **75**
© Carson-Dellosa CD-2205

Page 76 — Computerized Card Catalog

Name _____ Computerized Card Catalog

Refer to the sample card catalog entry to answer each question. Circle the letter beside the correct answer.

Title: *Buffalo Hunt*
Author: Freedman, Russell
Published: Holiday House, 1988
Physical description: 52 pp.
Notes: Examines the importance of the buffalo in the lore and day-to-day life of the Indian tribes of the Great Plains and describes hunting methods and the uses found for each part of the animal that could not be eaten.
Notes: Interest grade level: 3-7
Subject: Nonfiction
Subject: Animals

1. According to the card catalog, what do we know about the book?
   A. The book is about the Great Plains Indians.
   (B) This book is about the importance of buffalo to the Great Plains Indians.
   C. This book describes farming methods of the Great Plains Indians.
   D. This book describes stories told by the Great Plains Indians.

2. The person who wrote *Buffalo Hunt* is:
   A. Running Press   B. Holiday House   C. Great Plains   **(D) Russell Freedman**

3. How many pages does the book contain?
   A. 1988 pages   B. 37 pages   **(C) 52 pages**   D. 528 pages

4. For what grade level is the book intended?
   A. 2-4 grades   B. 5-8 grades   C. 1-9 grades   **(D) 3-7 grades**

5. What is the name of the publishing company?
   (A) Holiday House   B. Great Plains   C. Running Press   D. Russell Freedman

76 Total Problems: Total Correct: Score: © Carson-Dellosa CD-2205

Name _____   Reader's Guide to Literature/Title Page

Refer to the sample entry from *Reader's Guide to Literature* to answer each question. Circle the letter beside the correct answer.

> Taming Maggie [separation anxiety in dogs] S. Schultz. il *U.S. News & World Report*
> v.126 no.8 p.62-4 Mr 1 '99

1. What is the name of the article in the entry above?
   A. "Separation Anxiety in Dogs"   B. "U.S. News & World Report"
   (C) "Taming Maggie"   D. "S. Schultz"

2. Where is the article found, according to the entry above?
   A. S. Schultz   (B) *U.S. News & World Report*
   C. Separation Anxiety in Dogs   D. Taming Maggie

3. In which month and year is the article found?
   A. May 1999   B. May 1962
   (C) March 1999   D. March 1962

Refer to the sample title page entry to answer each question.

> **For the Love of Dogs**
>
> Kim Campbell Thornton
> Virginia Parker Guidry
>
> Publications International, Ltd.

4. Publications International, Ltd., is the name of the:
   A. author   (B) publisher
   C. book   D. city

5. Who wrote the book?
   A. Kim Thornton
   (B) Kim Thornton and Virginia Guidry
   C. Virginia Guidry
   D. Kenneth Thornton and Virginia Campbell

© Carson-Dellosa CD-2205

Total Problems:	Total Correct:	Score:

77

Name _____   Index

Refer to the sample index to answer each question. Circle the letter beside the correct answer.

> **INDEX**
> Fleas, 132,133
> Fleming's classification of dogs, 313, 314
> Folding portable dog pens, 53
> Follicles, 149
> Food, See also Diet.
> Food poisoning antidote, 142
> Food substitutes for chewing, 32
> Food supplements, 30
> "Foot," as coursing term, 189
> Foot care, 43
> "Force" retrieving, 239
> Foreign breeds, 331-337
>   Australian Cattle Dog, 331
>   Australian Kelpie, 331
>   Bichon Frise, 330
>   Chinook, 332
>   Chinese Crested Dog, 332
>   Catalan Sheepdog, 331
>   Drentsche Partrijshond, 332
>   Finnish Spitz, 333
>   Istrian Pointer, 333
>   Lurcher Dog, 333
>   Marenna Sheepdog, 333
>   Portuguese Pointer, 333
>   Rumanian Sheepdog, 333
>   Sealydale Terrier, 333
>   Spinone Dog, 333
>   Svensk-Valhund, 333
>   Tibetan Mastiff, 334
>   Wheaten Terrier, 335
> Foreign travel, 56-61
> Formula, See Milk.
> Fossils of early dogs, 282, 283

1. Suppose you wanted to find information on the Rumanian Sheepdog. On what page would you look?
   A. 331
   B. 337
   (C) 333
   D. 332

2. What is the main category or main heading found on pages 331-337?
   A. Catalan Sheepdog
   B. Australian Cattle Dog
   (C) Foreign Breeds
   D. Australian Kelpie

3. Beside the category "Food," there is a statement "See also Diet." This is called a cross reference. This means that:
   (A) One can also find information on food by looking under the main category "Diet."
   B. One can only find information on food by looking under "Food."
   C. There is no available information on food under the category "Food."
   D. There is no information available on food under "Food" or "Diet."

4. If your dog chews the furniture in your house and you wanted to find information on chewing, you could look on what page?
   A. 142
   (B) 32
   C. 332
   D. not available

78

Total Problems:	Total Correct:	Score:

© Carson-Dellosa CD-2205